Agile Human Resources

Agile Human Resources

Creating a Sustainable Future for the HR Profession

Kelly Swingler

BEP BUSINESS EXPERT PRESS

First published in 2018 by
Business Expert Press, LLC
222 East 46th Street, New York, NY 10017
www.businessexpertpress.com

ISBN-13: 978-1-94744-133-0 (paperback)
ISBN-13: 978-1-94744-134-7 (e-book)

Business Expert Press Human Resource Management and Organizational Behavior Collection

Collection ISSN: 1946-5637 (print)
Collection ISSN: 1946-5645 (electronic)

Cover and interior design by S4Carlisle Publishing Services
Private Ltd., Chennai, India

First edition: 2018

10 9 8 7 6 5 4 3 2 1

Printed in the United States of America.

Abstract

Over the last 20 years, the topic of conversation when it comes to HR, is whether or not it should even exist. The name of the function is ever changing, but are the outcomes and results evolving in the right way?

Over the last 5 years, Kelly Swingler has been designing and implementing HR solutions focused on doing things differently, and the creation of her AGILE HR framework is well received by all of her clients. Agile HR helps organizations manage, motivate, engage, inspire, and lead their people in the best possible way by treating them, first and foremost, as able adults that come to work to do a good job.

Mainstream HR, however, works from the perspective of policing employees through policies and procedures that suffocate and restrict employees and hinder creativity and innovation at work.

This book provides hints, tips, and examples of how to implement Agile HR solutions into your organization that will help HR professionals and senior leaders implement people-focused solutions to increase productivity.

It is time to put the human touch back into Human Resources.

Keyword

HR, employees, Agile HR, recruitment, leadership, management, talent management, onboarding, employee engagement, learning and development, employee reward, well-being

Contents

Chapter 1   Introduction 1
Chapter 2   Why HR Needs to Change? 5
Chapter 3   Introduction to AGILE HR 21
Chapter 4   Employee Life Cycle...25
Chapter 5   Overarching Factors 71
Chapter 6   Putting It into Practice 81
Chapter 7   Diagnostic Introduction...85
Chapter 8   Case Studies 93
Chapter 9   Resources 103
Chapter 10 Summary—Reflections 105
Index *107*

CHAPTER 1

Introduction

First, thank you for buying this book. I'm so pleased that you are interested in doing HR differently and that you want to create a sustainable future for the HR profession.

When I started in HR, I was passionate about wanting to create better places to work, where I did not have to sit at the pub, or in the hairdressers' and hear about the problems that my friends, friends of friends, and family were having at work—the difficulties they faced with managers, the long-winded and policy-driven ways of doing HR, and what I call the *Monday to Friday dying syndrome,* where you spend all week at work waiting for the weekend, and then, do the same the week after, and the week after that.

You have heard about it or experienced it yourself, right?

Monday – The dread of going to work fills you from head to toe. You drag yourself out of bed, and are already counting down the days until the weekend. You arrive at work, you cannot focus. People ask you if you have had a good weekend, and you say things such as, "Yes, great, thanks, but it wasn't long enough." It is not a productive day. You have got the rest of the week to get done what you need to get done.

Tuesday – Thank goodness, it is not Monday anymore; the week is moving forward. You start to really think about all of the things that you need to complete that week. Then, you spend the afternoon clearing your emails. Research has shown that marketing emails have the greatest chance of success if sent on Tuesday afternoons!

Wednesday (Or "Humpday") – You have survived the week so far; you are halfway there and already thinking about what you will be doing at the weekend. You have a lot of meetings today; everyone must be feeling the same way. You push through.

Thursday – Mad rush. Everything needs to be completed today, or so it appears. It is a last-minute rush to achieve what needs to be achieved by the end of the week. Why does it always feel like your organizations leaves things until the last minute? You stay late as you have lots to get through (if only you had made better use of the earlier part of the week!).

Friday – Woohoo, it's the weekend. You fly through your work, or look at what can wait until next week. Maybe you can leave the office early; after all, you have so much to plan and do for the weekend and you could do with getting out early. You take a longer lunch. You watch the clock and you can finally escape.

Saturday – What a great day—no work!

Sunday – Great day, but you cannot get the thoughts out of your head that you are back to work tomorrow. Oh, no!

Another week, the cycle repeats, over and over and over again.

We spend more than half our lives at work—more than half. And yet, many of us go through this cycle over and over again, and it needs to change.

The more I progressed and the more senior I got, it was more and more visible that the reasons these policies—and the Monday-to-Friday dying—were happening was because senior leaders did not trust their staff, their managers, and had little respect for the HR function. And HR functions were implementing policies and procedures in the hope of making a difference to the organization and gaining credibility from senior leaders, but usually without taking into account what managers—and more importantly, what employees—actually wanted.

When you think of the HR function in your organization, do you think of them being flexible, adaptable, speedy, and responsive?

No. Nor do many other companies, and sadly, HR is the one department that shoulders the blame and nobody bats an eyelid. "It's HR's fault" is common parlance.

The reality is that much of the time, it is not HR's fault; managers are not managing, leaders are not leading, but instead of HR looking at why people are not following procedures or trying to simplify policies to make them easy to implement, much of what we have created over the years as part of our training and development—and based on the management tools designed in the 1980s—is not fit for purpose. It is not agile; it does not make things easy for people; and it does not empower anyone in the workplace.

When I was appointed as the UK's Youngest HR Director, I was convinced I could make a BIG change in the way that HR designed and implemented solutions, and I could change the perception of the HR function. I believe that in the right company, I could have achieved this, but I realized that for me, in order to truly drive change, to start doing HR differently, and to help my clients do the same, without them wasting time or money, I needed to start my own consultancy.

In 2013, I left my corporate HR role and started my own consultancy with a passion for—and a commitment to—creating better places to work and practice HR, learning, and leadership differently.

My company has gone from strength to strength over the last 4 years, and I am now delighted that our approach and some of the new ways of thinking from Silicon Valley, other forward-thinking organizations in the UK, and consultancies such as HR Disrupted have been brought together in this book, along with our online program, workshop, and diagnostic tool.

So, what will this book cover?

We will look first at why HR needs changing, and then, I will introduce you to the AGILE model, before we move onto the employee lifecycle and see how AGILE HR fits into this.

We will then look at the overarching factors to consider before we move on to the future being Agile and how you can start to create and implement change in your own organizations.

You will also find throughout the book that you will be introduced to case studies and examples of new ways of thinking, tools and resources, videos, audios, and some questions to get you thinking.

You can dip in and out of the book at any point to suit you, although I do recommend starting from the beginning and working through it at your own pace, and then, dipping in and out as and when you need to, to help you create sustainable change.

If you have attended one of the workshops or completed the online program, then do use this book as a resource tool to keep your learning fresh, and I hope you will also learn something new as you progress through.

There is also plenty of opportunity for you to make use of the online community of like-minded professionals that are in the HR Hub to test and share your thinking and ideas, so do say Hi, interact and collaborate as much as you can. As social creatures and social learners, this can help improve your experience no end.

I hope you enjoy the book; a lot of love, thought, and creativity have gone into it and I look forward to hearing your thoughts as you move through it.

And now, if you are ready to start doing HR differently, let us get started.

Happy reading ☺

CHAPTER 2

Why HR Needs to Change?

Since the management thinking of the 1970s, 1980s, and 1990s, lifestyles, businesses, technology, and people themselves have changed, yet our ways of working have not. Since starting my career in HR in the late 1990s, we have changed our designation—Personnel, HR, and now, we are starting to move into the designation "People," and even—as I saw recently—Head of Employee Happiness. Yet, with these name changes and new buzzwords such as "Employee Engagement," for the most part, we still recruit, induct, train, develop, pay, and promote our people in much the same way.

And it is simply not working.

Treating employees as individuals is a big part of AGILE HR also, yet we continue to create one-size-fits-all approaches to managing and developing our people.

People want to work with more flexibility, more autonomy; they want to be creative and recognized for their hard work and efforts. They want to be thanked for doing a good job and have goals and objectives that are relevant. They do not want to fear being disciplined or dismissed for making a mistake, but be given the opportunity and support to learn from these. Our people want to be treated like people, not numbers, and they want us to care.

And yet, our policies—from dress code, to working from home (WFH), to how to book and take your annual leave, how to record sickness absence, and how you will rate on your performance review—are not what people want.

Will some employees push the boundaries as much as possible if you are more lenient, or if you trust them more, or give them greater accountability?

Possibly, yes.

But, we have to give it a try.

I know people that string work out all of the time to make it last as long as possible, who arrive late, always take their hour for lunch, and then, leave early all of the time, who want to do the bare minimum, day in and day out. These people will not last long in my organization or under my leadership because that is not the way we do things around here.

And if you have these people in your organization, then what is needed is more effective adult-to-adult conversations that take place on a regular basis, or bigger projects, or tighter deadlines, and certainly, more effective management if this style of working bothers you.

What is needed is more effective management, and more effective leadership and HR processes, policies, and procedures that support the leadership of the organization. A new HR policy is not the answer to someone becoming more effective at work.

What we *can* do is make sure that our HR practices are not pages and pages and pages of jargon and micromanagement guidelines that set boundaries so tight that people cannot breathe; they need to be simple and easy to digest.

I started a new position with a company where all of the policies were so long and complicated that even with over 10 years of experience, I could neither understand the steps that had already been taken nor advise them on what to do next. In my first week, I was handed a complex employee relations case; it had everything in it from performance issues, complaints, harassment, bullying, fraud and conspiracy allegations and had been going on for months. The people who had been dealing with it previously had left and I was asked to pick up the pieces. It was a minefield. I met with the people concerned, and started the process again. It was resolved quickly, and while not to everyone's satisfaction, it came to a conclusion, but I had to practically ignore the policy in order to make things happen.

As we move to more or even totally online working, we can work from anywhere, literally anywhere, and as long as we get the job done, what does it matter what is in a policy? Yet, I have seen so many WFH policies that make me shudder, that the thought of WFH would terrify me into going into the office every day, where I can hot-desk at the same desk that I have always used, not really engage with anyone, and then, go home again.

Organizations are always looking for ways to do more for less, to save costs and drive efficiencies. Technology has changed the way we work, live, and think, and who knows what the future political landscape will look like and how it will impact businesses and our people?

But even with all of this change and uncertainty going on in the world in which we live and work, HR has changed very little, and if we do not change, I do not believe we have a future.

Radical change—and some of what we will cover *will* sound radical— or even any change, for that matter, does not happen overnight; it will take time. You are likely to be challenged (a lot), possibly even have your ideas rubbished because they have not been proven elsewhere, and of course, there is going to be a risk involved with presenting something new in the first place, but also, in the design, implementation, and then, sustaining the change.

Most, or at least some of the managers and leaders, in your organization will welcome the changes, and may even wonder why you did not implement them years ago; others will fight against you as it is not "the way we do things," but what may be your biggest challenge is changing your own mindset and that of your team, because after all, the policies, procedures, processes, and policing are our creation. The HR profession has taught us that this is the way we have to do things and we risk being taken to court if anything goes wrong or people get upset, and we would not have created all of this paperwork, and processes, and policies, and procedures if they were not needed, right?

Wrong.

Most of what we have designed has come from an outdated HR model, and when I say outdated, I am not talking 30 years ago. Even some of the research carried out in 2008 is no longer relevant for HR, and yet, we still use it.

To add to this, new employment legislation that comes into force because one company treated someone badly, or was accused and lost the case despite not doing anything wrong, causes us to write yet another policy, and tighten up even more on the way we lead, manage, and engage our people.

And if your organization has been threatened with or lost an Employment Tribunal case, then the chances are the HR function is seen as one internal police force ensuring that every single conversation is documented and signed by both parties and that no manager or employee has any wiggle room at all when it comes to speaking with one another.

So, this has to change. And the good news is, when it is changed and it is working well, it is amazing!

I am involved in many online HR communities and some face-to-face groups, many of which are challenging the old-school styles of HR and thinking outside the box. But so, so many continue to focus on complicated, outdated policies with no relevance in the world of work as it is today. And, I am sad to say, most of this comes down to leaders asking for more and more policies because of one issue that is happening in the workplace, and rather than manage this appropriately, they insist on a new policy being written and implemented to tar everyone with the same brush.

And HR do not question this. We do not appear to be pushing back, or asking why this policy is needed, or finding another, better way to handle things. We run off to write a policy, asking others in our networks if they have one we can borrow, piece something together, and implement, either in isolation or through our employee forums.

And what is more, when the wider workforce ask why this is needed, we give the one example of where it has happened, and say it is needed to prevent anything similar from happening again.

The policies I have seen—and my sincere apologies for some of the ones my teams and I have written—do not allow people to feel empowered, valued, and trusted.

For those of you reading this that are parents, can you imagine punishing your child each time they tried something new? Or disciplining them each time they fell off their bike, or tried to walk, or spilled food, or made a mess, or did not come first in their race? Yet, this is what we do in the workplace.

And we think that because we are paying people, we have control over everything they do, and limit them doing anything that is not in a policy or procedure.

I read just this week that one of my previous CEOs has resigned from his position. The reasons given in the two press releases that I saw related to incomplete work, issues with finances, and a lack of challenge at the Board level, meaning it was his word only. He led with everything needing to be done *his* way. When a colleague and I challenged him once on the way employees were being treated, we were both told that we were "HR professionals with ideas above their remit who should just do what we were told as we had no idea about business." I have proved that statement wrong on many occasions, but sadly, this is how HR are seen.

We have to change this if we want the profession—whatever we decide to call ourselves—to have a future.

I know that when we pay attention to the needs of the business, and the needs of the people in the business, that HR can add value, bucket-loads of it; it is time we started to prove this on a global scale.

Before we go into the detail of the book and help you understand more of the neuroscience behind our thought patterns, why we find change difficult and how fear is created, we discuss mindset in this next part so that you can start to see what you need to do personally to start changing mindsets—your own and of those around you, especially of the leaders in your organization.

2.1   An Introduction to Mindset

How the Brain Works and Why We Think and Feel the Way We Do

Before we go into some of the specifics about how to change the way we design and deliver HR solutions, let us start with a bit more of the science behind why our people can feel the way they do.

As you read through this part of the book, consider these three questions:

- Do your existing HR practices instill fear?
- Do your existing HR practices encourage social interaction?
- Do your existing HR practices encourage the feeling of reward?

Ok, so let us start by understanding how the brain works; how we create feelings of doubt, fear, stress, anxiety, lack of confidence, and phobic responses; how the interference comes and goes and what we can do about it; and why some existing working practices and management practices do not encourage the feeling of happiness at work or get the best out of your people.

If we imagine our brain to be the shape of a rugby ball, the very tip at the front of the ball is called the prefrontal cortex—this is to the bit you know as YOU.

It is your conscious part, the part that interacts with the world; the part we are using to be aware of our interactions together. At the moment, it is attached to a vast intellectual resource, the intellectual mind (the top part of the ball). This part, we do not share with other animals.

Now, when we operate from the intellectual part of the brain, we generally get things right in life. It will always come up with answers based on a proper assessment of the situation and is generally very positive.

There is another part of the brain. This part is the original primitive part (the bottom of the ball). The central and influential part of this brain is the amygdala. This is generally referred to as the fight/flight/depression area of the brain and is associated with two other very primitive parts— the hippocampus, which holds all our primitive, and sometimes, inappropriate behavioral experiences and patterns, and the hypothalamus, which regulates chemical responses in the body and mind.

So, let us imagine that when you leave the room you are sat in today, you run into a polar bear.

What would happen?

Your anxiety would go up. You would lose intellectual control and move from the top part of the brain (the intellectual brain) to the bottom part of the brain (the primitive emotional brain), go "sweaty," increasing the heartbeat, churning the stomach, and you would be off like a shot.

In the circumstances, this response would be entirely appropriate and you would be pleased.

Unfortunately, it is the same in life. When our anxiety goes up—and it can be a gradual process—we lose intellectual control and to a greater or lesser extent, the primitive mind takes over and this mind always operates within the primitive parameters of depression, anxiety, and anger, or a combination of all three.

If our primitive mind thinks that, for one reason or another, our life is in some sort of crisis or emergency, it will step in generally to help.

Depression, anxiety, and anger are all primitive opt-out clauses.

When the caveman looked out of the cave and there was snow, or ice, or danger, and he could not go out to hunt, he pulled the rug over his head and did not interact until the situation changed. We have adapted this to all the modern-day symptoms of depression, anxiety, and stress, and in a work context, this is what we might call a "duvet day" or when people throw a "sickie."

If we were in the jungle in those days, I doubt very much if we would be too far away from our panic button at any given time.

And anger is merely a primitive way of increasing our strength to defend ourselves against wild animals and other wild tribesmen, and in many cases, it is this increase in anxiety that creates our thoughts of fear, stress, self-doubt, or phobias.

But there is more.

The primitive mind is a negative mind. It will always see things from the worst possible perspective. If you think about it, it has to for your self-preservation. When you run into the polar bear, your mind will not say, "Ah, it has probably eaten." No, quite rightly, it will say, "It will snaffle you."

This response is great when we run into polar bears, but not so good when the bank statement arrives, or we are facing redundancy, or we have had an argument, and so on.

It is an obsessional mind. If you did have a polar bear in the back garden, you would be reminded of it constantly. You would keep checking.

It is a vigilant mind. If the perception is that danger is all around, then it is wise to stay on red alert.

And, because the primitive brain is not an intellectual one, it cannot be innovative. It has to refer to previous patterns of behavior. If what we did yesterday ensured our survival, then we are encouraged to do it again.

So, think about your workplace.

Are you encouraging a stressful place to work in? Do your people understand what is required of them? Are they supported during change? Do your managers and leaders lead from a place of fear, where every action they take is under scrutiny, and it is only a matter of time before you are telling them, "You're fired"?

How do we create this anxiety that causes us to move from the intellectual, sensible part of the brain to the angry, anxious, and depressed part?

Well, anxiety is caused by negative thinking.

It is not the events in one's lives that necessarily cause the perception of crisis. No, if that were so, everyone at university would be suffering from panic attacks, and we know that is not the case. So, it must be our thought patterns surrounding the events of our life.

Every negative thought we have is converted into anxiety. We can create anxiety by negatively forecasting the future, about big things—"We will never be able to afford that", "I'll never find another girlfriend," "I'll never have a baby," and so on. It can be small things, like that meeting.

Here, we should remember that the mind cannot tell the difference between imagination and reality.

Intellectually, you know the meeting is going to go OK; they generally do, but being you, you start thinking about things going wrong.

You think about it 50 times?

The actual meeting goes quite well, but you have attended 51 meetings and 50 have been disasters.

We can negatively introspect about the past.

Now, within the primitive mind, there is a library of all the patterns of thought and patterns of behavior that help us to survive.

Some of them are instinctive, but a baby does not know where it is going to be born—the Antarctic, or the jungle, for example.

So, it needs to be able to learn automatic patterns of thought and behavior, based on its environment.

So, when a 3-year-old primitive is faced with a bear for the first time, he has to be able to learn that that bear is not something nice and big, fluffy to play with; the mind has to learn that that bear is going to eat the 3-year-old primitive unless he gets the hell out of there.

And it learns that because mum is screaming, "BEAR!!" The 3-year-old primitive child picks up the stress from mum, focuses on the bear, and forms that pattern in the primitive mind that says, "Bears are dangerous."

So, next time he is out in the forest, he is keeping a look out for bears. If he spots one, the primitive mind refers to the pattern that says bears are dangerous, and gets him the hell out of there with the fight or flight response.

This releases adrenaline and cortisol into the bloodstream, which increases the heart rate and breathing rate and blood pressure to get oxygen to his muscles, which then enable him to escape as quickly as possible.

But sometimes, the subconscious gets it wrong.

You can imagine Daisy, aged 1, is playing with a spider on the carpet when mum walks in, who has always been terrified of spiders. Mum screams because Daisy's eating the damn thing by this stage and Daisy forms that pattern that says, "Spiders are dangerous."

Meanwhile, during these potentially dangerous situations, the logical rational mind gets blocked out—partly because the subconscious is trying to protect those patterns that it thinks are important for survival, and partly because logic is just too slow. If you meet a bear, the last thing you want is to rationally analyze what kind of a bear it is, whether it is dangerous, whether it is hungry, or whether you should freeze or run like hell.

This is why Daisy, 20 years down the line, logically and rationally knows that spiders are not dangerous in this country—but that does not stop her primitive mind not letting her in the same room as a spider.

So, here is this distinction between what she logically and rationally knows to be the case and the behavior that the subconscious drives.

Now, imagine the spider is one of the managers in your workplace and you know that some of your people dread meeting with them. Or, it is the board meeting where you got shot down last time you made a suggestion and have not wanted to talk in the room since. Or, you have a group of people who are so terrified of speaking up and giving presentations because they forgot what they were saying last time or the presentation did not work for them!

Every negative thought that we have is accumulated and stored. We say it is stored in a stress bucket. Thankfully, we do have a method for emptying our bucket and it is known as REM sleep—rapid eye movement.

At night, we re-run events of the day and change them from being an emotional memory to a narrative memory, a memory that we have control over.

You are familiar with how REM works. Someone upsets you in the afternoon and you really are upset. You tell your partner and they say, "Forget about it," but you really cannot. You are thinking about it when you go to bed.

During your REM sleep, you will re-run the event, either clearly or metaphorically (dreaming), and you will move it from the primitive brain to the intellectual brain, where you have control over it.

So, when you awaken in the morning, you might well have forgotten about the wretched person; or you might not, but you will certainly be saying something such as, "How do I allow these people to upset me so?"

I fondly imagine that I awaken each morning with my bucket emptied, so I can start the day without anxiety, anger, depression, or fear.

You do not. Why?

Well, here, depending on whether you have too much or too little REM sleep, there are two scenarios.

Scenario 1

For a start, you have been piling too much into your bucket. (Sometimes, it will overflow!) Sadly, for one reason or another, REM is restricted to about 20 percent of our sleep patterns.

If we try and overdo that, then the mind will wake you up. You know when it is your mind waking you up because you wake up wide awake, and often, feel quite miserable.

Often, we cannot get back to sleep again. You know the difference between that and the baby waking you up, for instance.

Now, we are in the grip of a bit of a vicious circle. The more you have in your bucket, the more time you will spend in your primitive brain, and the more you will be encouraged to be negative.

So, to get you back on top of things, you need to restrict the amount you are piling into your bucket, and get you concentrating on the positive things in your life.

You will know when you are doing this when you start sleeping better.

Scenario 2

You are still piling too much into your bucket and it takes a great deal of effort to attempt to empty it.

Sadly, REM is enervating. It has enormous energy in that effort to diffuse that anxiety.

Sometimes, we can overdo it and this exhausts us and makes us even more low, anxious, or fearful.

Now, we find ourselves in the grip of a vicious circle again.

In an attempt to empty our bucket in this scenario, we are encouraged to sleep more and more; sometimes all day, which makes our depression, anxiety, stress, or fear worse and worse.

So again, you need to restrict the amount you are piling into your bucket, and get yourself concentrating on the positive aspects in your life.

You need to reorganize your sleep patterns too.

On the Chrysalis Consulting website, under the Learning Lounge section, you will find an audio link for relaxation. You can use this once a day for the next few weeks, or as long as you like, perhaps just when needed, to help improve your sleep, increase your REM, and get you operating more effectively from the rational and logical part of your brain when fearful or stressful situations occur.

I just want to tell you about the physiology before we move on, about what happens in the brain when we suffer from anxiety disorders, depression, and fear.

Early men and early women were given quite definite rewards for carrying out certain evolutionary processes.

They got a reward when they hunted and gathered, and successfully supported themselves and their families.

We are better as a tribe rather than individuals, and they got rewarded when they interacted with others.

The reward they got were quite definitely recognized and scientists are adamant about this.

They felt motivated.

But most of all, it was a coping mechanism; it helped them cope with day-to-day activities, helped them cope better with physical fear, made them braver; it even helped them cope with physical pain.

No doubt they were pleased.

Now, we know what that reward is.

It is a chemical response in the brain that produces various neurotransmitters that act as catalysts for that sort of mentally healthy behavior.

And you know, the neurotransmitter we talk about most—simply because it is the most important—is serotonin, the happy hormone.

When we produce a constant flow of serotonin, we are nice, happy, coping, brave little souls!

So, we need to operate within these positive parameters like early man, and although we do not have to go out to hunt, we do have to interact in a positive way, be active in a positive way, and think in a positive way (the 3 Ps).

Because when we do, we produce patterns in the brain that give us that constant flow of serotonin.

Take some time now to consider patterns, and behaviors, or events that create a negative and physical reaction in you.

Now, go back to three questions I asked you to consider at the beginning of this section:

- Do your existing HR practices instil fear?
- Do your existing HR practices encourage social interaction?
- Do your existing HR practices encourage the feeling of reward?

Right from when we are at school, we are taught that competing with others is what we need to do in order to survive, and this is played out even more in the workplace. Collaboration and social interaction is not seen as a great way to build businesses, and yet, they are a huge part of what we need as people, and do encourage productivity.

Many HR, management, and leadership practices, though, do all they can to divide and conquer. You will only get your bonus if you are better than everyone else. You will only get the job if you can talk about your own successes and ignore how you led, motivated, and engaged your team. You will only get your pay increase if you can demonstrate how well you have performed. You will only get your promotion if you can prove just how determined you are to succeed and you do not care how many people you have to trample on along the way.

This type of fear-driven leadership is no longer effective in the workplace, and yet, so many of our HR practices still drive this type of behavior, and then, talk about the importance of employee well-being and employee engagement in another policy. The two do not gel particularly well and it is no wonder so many of our employees are confused and live the repeated weekly cycle of Monday-to-Friday dying syndrome.

2.2   Masculine and Feminine Leadership Traits

I mentioned earlier that much of the way we design and deliver HR solutions remains embedded still in the management thinking of the 1970s, 1980s, and 1990s, and that this is no longer sustainable.

The world of business is changing, the world is changing, and if you tap into what all of the spiritualists are telling us, we are moving into the age of the feminine.

John Gerzema completed some research and included the findings of this in his book "The Athena Doctrine: How Women (And The Men Who Think Like Them) Will rule the future," and this showed that many of the leadership traits that we still encourage in organizations are masculine leadership traits. In order for business and people to thrive in the current world and in the future, it was found that we need to adopt more of the feminine leadership traits.

I include this thinking in the book because I believe we need a blend of both masculine and feminine thinking, planning, and execution in order to live a balanced life, be happy in our work, and run successful organizations that focus, first and foremost, on how they lead, manage, and engage their people, and HR has a huge and vital role in driving this change forward.

The Athena Doctrine provides a lot of in-depth research and thinking, demonstrating that businesses and leaders need to be more feminine in order for businesses to succeed (I will leave you to make your own mind up on that). It is not about men or women being better than one another, but about the traits that need to be developed and more visible in business.

What I know is that men started many big companies with billions of pounds of income each year many years ago. I also know that when people try to railroad me or bully me, or undermine me at work, both men or women, I do not take kindly to this.

So, you will find the following table outlining the "traits" of the masculine and feminine, and I know I have a blend of the two. I am not going to go into too much detail on this as you will know the traits you have in order to live the life you want and to develop your career and your HR functions.

For example, I am very imaginative and creative, but if all I do is imagine and create without a plan or an outcome in mind, how will I generate income? I do work I truly love, but I have to keep a constant reality check going to make sure I am on the right path, even though I live my life largely by intuition.

Feminine	Masculine
Heart	Mind
Feeling	Thinking
Passive	Active
Stillness and resting	Being in the world
Receptive	Directive
Imagination	Reason
Creativity	Logical and linear thinking
Formlessness	Structure
Intuition and the unknown	Logic and certainty
Innocence "in no sense"	Must "make sense"
Nurturing	Orientating
Passionate	Decisive
Intuitive	Resilient
Flexible	Analytical
Plans for the future	Aggressiveness
Loyal	Proud
Reasonable	Arrogance
Collaborative	Independent
Selfless	Selfish
Empathetic	Individualistic
What you truly love	What you think you need
Living for joy	Living to survive
Vision	Reality
Just being is valid	Must achieve to be valid
Beauty	Will
Soft	Hard
Internal	External
Attraction	Assertion
Collective	Individual
Flexible	Rigid
Flow	Go
Process	Outcome

WHY HR NEEDS TO CHANGE? 19

As I touched on briefly earlier, I believe a blend is important, balance is key, and as we see in Yin and Yang, we cannot solely have one thing without a small proportion of the other.

But if you think about the HR practices, policies, and procedures that are in your organization, which side of the previous table do they tend to focus on?

If I were to hazard a guess, I would say mostly the masculine side. How is that working for your people? For your business success? How many employee relations issues are you currently dealing with? How much sickness absence are you currently operating with? Is stress high at work? Do your people love working with you? Would they recommend your organization as a great place to work in? What about your retention?

Monday-to-Friday dying syndrome, anyone?

Now, of course, passion is great, but if nobody is making any decisions, that is not great for business of your people. Someone will, of course, also need to be analyzing the data, but if overanalyzing and never making a decision stops you from being flexible and planning for the future, then it is unlikely that your business will survive.

Before we start to look at the AGILE approach to HR, take some time now and consider the type of organization you want to create and how HR can help shape, inform, and lead on doing things differently. Consider things such as how your people will feel, how they will interact with one another, how the leaders and managers engage with their people, how people feel when they enter the building and say good morning to each other.

On the Chrysalis Consulting website, you will find a guided visualization, "The Perfect Organisation," to help you with this activity, if needed.

When finished, keep this in mind as you work through the rest of the book to find the solutions that are right for your people, your leaders and your organization through the AGILE approach to HR.

Additional points to consider:

- Know what it takes to make your HR function work.
- Know what your customers need.
- Know where you need to adapt and grow—Take steps to make it happen.
- Identify where you need help—and then, get it.

CHAPTER 3

Introduction to AGILE HR

Agile

ˈadʒʌɪl/
adjective

1.
   able to move quickly and easily.
   "Ruth was as agile as a monkey."

2.
   relating to or denoting a method of project management, used especially
   for software development, that is characterized by the division of tasks
   into short phases of work and frequent reassessment and adaptation
   of plans.
   "agile methods replace high-level design with frequent redesign"

Agile, as you can see, is basically about being able to move quickly and easily and adapting plans.

If anyone in your organization refers to your HR function as adaptable, agile, and moving quickly and easily, you can stop reading, because you have already got it sorted. These are not usually terms that describe many HR functions, policies, or procedures on the whole, but they can be.

Interestingly, a few months ago, when I was delivering a talk to a group of HR students, I asked them what they thought their role was. All of them said it was about ensuring people followed and adhered to the policies and procedures. Wow, what an inspiring role!

So, what is AGILE HR and how can it make a difference to the way you lead, manage, and engage your people?

AGILE is recognizing, and then, treating your employees as:

- Able
- Game-changers
- Individuals
- Leaders and
- Engaged

And when you get this right, your people feel engaged, performance improves, and you have happier staff and happier customers.

Great words, but what do they mean in principle?

Employees that are Able – This is where you recognize that your employees come to work to do a good job—where you feel you can trust them to do a good job and not have to police them constantly. It is trusting that they perform to the best of their ability and that they can work with autonomy in a flexible way and still get done what they need to, when they need to.

Employees that are Game-changers – Your employees are where the majority of your ideas, creativity, and innovation can come from. They know what works well and what needs to be changed. Involve them in the way you do things and reap the benefits.

Employees that are Individuals – For too long, we have been creating a one-size-fits-all approach to policies, procedures, programs, and processes, and then, wondering why nobody follows them. If you start by recognizing that your employees have different wants, needs, and drivers, then you are onto a winner.

Employees that are Leaders – Leaders within a business are too often seen as only those that hold the most senior positions, but this is not the case. Leaders are those that are able to lead, engage, and develop others within the business, no matter what their job title or status. They are self-starters and have the best interests of the business at heart.

Employees that are Engaged – It is about shared values, a shared vision, and a shared purpose. This is much, much more than an annual survey. This is about what your employees will say about you to their family and friends at the pub after work. If you can give them (within a framework) the space to work in a way that suits them, that encourages their ideas, that recognizes them as an individuals and allows them to lead, they will be engaged, and engaged and happy staff lead to engaged and happy customers. It's win-win.

AGILE HR places the employee at the heart of their employment journey. The HR function becomes an enabler of change and development while the managers support and develop their people. The employee becomes more responsible for their objectives, for their performance management, for their learning and development, for their career progression. The employee takes ownership and works with autonomy.

This enables managers to manage and HR to focus more on growth and organizational development.

Before you go any further with this book, consider a project or initiative you are working on currently, or even your existing HR policies, and take some time to answer these questions:

- Does this allow space for our employees to demonstrate their ability in a trusting and autonomous way?
- Does this encourage ideas, creativity, and innovation for our people?
- Does it reflect that our people are individuals?
- Does it reflect that our people are leaders?
- Does it reflect where we all have a shared purpose, a shared vision, and shared values, and would it be something that our people would feel proud about sharing with their family and friends?

Take some time to answer these questions, discuss them your team, your senior leaders, and then, when you are ready, let us look at how AGILE HR works throughout the employee life cycle.

CHAPTER 4

Employee Life Cycle

The employee life cycle, or employee roadmap, includes all of the points at which you interact with your staff. You have the daily interactions and conversations, of course, that take place on a formal and informal basis, and many other departments may also have interactions with your people.

The life cycle are the stages of an employee's career from the point of initial engagement (attraction) to the point at which they finally depart the organization, for whatever reason (exit).

So, let us look now in some detail at each of the points in the life cycle of an employee and how an AGILE HR approach can benefit your people and your organization.

4.1 Recruitment

Recruitment starts way before we post job adverts or contact our preferred recruitment partner, and yet, at times, we forget this.

We make the assumption that just because we post a job advert, everyone will be falling at our feet to apply, because, well, it is a job, and why wouldn't people want to apply.

But as we know, when the job market is candidate-rich, we are likely to get a lot of applications from the "wrong" people and we spend a lot of time, money, and energy shortening the list of people to invite for an interview.

We then spend what can feel like a lifetime trying to get managers to commit to interview dates (and even then, they often cancel, and then, wonder why HR have let all of the "good" candidates go), and we interview, make an offer, and start the onboarding/induction process.

"I love recruiting people," said very few people, ever.

And how many people do you know that actually enjoy going through a recruitment process and get excited about being interviewed?

I have been through two great recruitment processes as a candidate in my career. Just two. And including my part time jobs while I was at school and college, I have worked for 11 companies.

So, what made only two of these stand out?

One of them involved an assessment center where, as candidates, we started off by introducing ourselves and giving a presentation, and then, the rest of the day was full of fun activities (with a purpose, obviously) before we each were asked to say who we had worked best with on the day and why, and then, who we had not worked well with and why.

I was 18, and this was my first experience of honest, open, and transparent feedback. Following the assessment center, we then spent the day with employees in the business, working on a series of exercises, and then, two formal interviews with four different senior managers.

It was not competency-based questioning, but questions based on why we had performed the way we had or why and how we felt we had worked well or not so well with people throughout the process and what we would change if we were in the same situation again.

The second one involved another group assessment center, less games, but lots of problems to solve and was facilitated by a psychologist. The second stage involved another full day with two psychologists and we worked alongside members of the HR team that we would be managing, and then, finally, we delivered a presentation to the CEO and were asked questions about the stages of the process so far and questions about our presentation.

No competency-based questions.

I will never forget these processes or the way I felt throughout them. As a candidate, I felt people were genuinely interested in me, that I was a person, and that I actually got the chance to demonstrate my strengths in different situations.

What was also apparent in these processes was that recruitment was important, and that recruiting the right people into the business was important, and that time and energy, and in some cases, quite a bit of money to ensure that the right people were selected was also important.

I did not, at any of these recruitment processes, feel like any of the panel members were bored or disengaged. I felt important and valued and I wanted to be part of this type of organization. Regardless of whether you were a successful candidate or not, you would have felt valued during each of these processes.

I have now seen two programs on TV about the recruitment process at LEGO, one when they were recruiting for designers for their head office and one when they were recruiting staff for their new London store.

I do not know many people that did not have LEGO in the house while they were growing up. I loved it as a child and so did my brother, and my sons loved it too. Even my brother-in-law in his 40s has a LEGO Ferrari on the shelf in his office. Essentially, of course, it is just plastic bricks, but the endless world of creativity, play, fun, and imagination is amazing; one of my favorites was the Millennium Falcon; it took hours, but we got there in the end.

The brand, the whole brand is about creativity and ideas. It is about passion. It is about excitement and getting busy with your hands. Can you imagine how all of that brand and passion could go to wreck and ruin if candidates were sat in room for a competency-based interview and then the second stage was another competency based interview.

Would you be inspired to work there still?

Where is the reflection of the brand in that process?

At Disneyworld, you are literally auditioned before being offered a job. Why?

Because they believe when you are at work, you are on stage. Your job is to make people enjoy the experience, to show fun, and laughter, and engagement with your customers.

A competency-based interview is not a substitute for being on stage.

If you want to be an employer of choice, where people really want to work for you, and you know you can gain the best candidates out there, start engaging with future employees now.

On your Work for Us page, include videos or testimonials from your people at all levels; invite people to follow you on social media platforms, and then, post videos about your people, your ethos, your leaders, and what is important to you.

When you have a vacancy or two, post a video telling the world about it and explain the process. If anyone has been turned off by what you have been posting, they will not want to work for you, and therefore, will not waste their time or yours in applying.

At Chrysalis Consulting, we have been able to create a portfolio of potential applicants that we keep in monthly contact with via blogs and e-mails that we can connect with and build a relationship with before even advertising a role. And if the role is not suitable for anyone in the community, they forward it on to people they know, and they already trust us and know what we do just by the manner in which we communicate with them.

Two films that I refer to when it comes to recruitment are *The Pursuit of Happiness* and *The Internship*. Internships are something very unusual in the UK, but used by many large companies in the U.S. and this trend is growing across the world. In the UK, our thinking is currently based on the fact that internships are free labor and do not add any benefit, which I hope may change soon, but I love the idea of internships and the films mentioned, while not primarily about recruitment, for People Professionals like me, I like them.

Both films tell very different stories, and involve very different characters, but what I love about them is the focus on building relationships, on collaborating, and on finding different approaches to working, and they both demonstrate that success is based on factors other than just numbers.

What is more, the length of the process and the expectations during the process allow both the employer and the employee to ascertain whether they are a good fit for one another.

Shouldn't every recruitment process be a two-way process?

Think back to the mindset section of the book and how we looked at how the brain works and why we feel the way we do.

Many recruitment processes focus on an application, an interview, possibly one assessment center, possibly a second interview, and then, an offer is made. We usually make a decision to recruit based on 2 or 3 hours in conversation with a person in an environment that does not reflect the true nature of the role, and at a time when their stress levels are likely through the roof.

To top it off, the interview panel are there because they "have" to be, the manager is too busy thinking about the e-mails that need to be answered or the project that needs completing today, and they say yes to the person that seemed most like them, because in a lot of cases, we are attracted to those who are most like us, while the rest of the panel is trying to ascertain cultural fit, fit with the team, and ability to do the job.

While with one of my employers, I carried out so many interviews for Tradesmen and Gas Engineers that I could have quite easily got the job because I grew to know what they were talking about, it would only be on Day One that my incompetence in these areas would have been identified. Likewise, I have interviewed finance and procurement directors so often that I could make a case for being recruited to manage contracts and suppliers and being able to set and drive finance strategy at a senior level while managing the expectations of stakeholders and the board. In reality, while I know enough of this to get by, I could not do the job.

What I am getting at here is that with enough practice, we can all get through a competency-based interview if we understand the role enough. But this type of environment does not really allow candidates to demonstrate their skills, or how they cope under pressure, or how they work with others, or how capable they are at making decisions or learning from mistakes, or analyzing information, or whatever else the role entails.

From the point of attracting people to your organization to the point that they join you for their first day, you need to be demonstrating that recruiting the right people in the right way and at the right time is important to you. You need to be engaging with candidates to allow them to show their skills, their qualities, and their strengths so that when you make a decision, you absolutely know you have recruited the best person, not just the person who was better at being interviewed.

If the best candidate has had traumatic interview experiences before, what are they thinking of as they enter the room? Yep, the last traumatic interview they had. And how will that have impacted their sleep the night before, or even their sleep over the last week? Will they be pumped up with happy hormones or stressed to the hill?

In the resources section at the back of the book, you will find examples from other organizations about what they do to attract and recruit the best people.

Before you move on, take some time and consider your own recruitment process.

- Does it reflect your brand?
- Would it excite you as a potential candidate?

- If you could wave a magic wand and create the best recruitment process for your organization, what would you create?
- How could you then implement this in your organization?

Then, answer:

- Does this allow candidates to demonstrate their ability?
- Does this encourage ideas, creativity, and innovation for candidates?
- Does it reflect that your candidates are individuals?
- Does it demonstrate that your people are leaders?
- Does it demonstrate that the candidates have a shared purpose, a shared vision, and shared values, and would it be something that they would feel proud about sharing with their family and friends?

Take some time to answer these questions and share your answers and reflections with your team, your leaders, or in the HR Hub on the Chrysalis website.

4.2   Onboarding/Induction

Onboarding is a common term used in the U.S. for the induction period (usually the first three to 6 months of a new employee's employment), and in the UK, I have heard it used as the part between the offer being made and the person actually joining; either way, none of these processes (onboarding or induction) sound particularly appealing.

As HR professionals, what typically happens as soon as we have offered you your dream job is that we send you enough paper (to kill a rainforest) to read and sign, telling you what you can and cannot do, mainly what you cannot do, to act as a doorstop and enough pieces of paper to sign to give you RSI (repetitive strain injury), all of which you must return before you start working at the organization or we probably won't pay you for your first month because, you know, our internal processes and form filling just takes far too long.

We look forward to you joining us soon, though.

However, please do not get too comfortable because we are going to review your performance in 6 months, and if we decide we do not like you, or that you are not doing what we want you to do, then we will let you go.

Of course, this will only happen if your manager remembers to do the meeting in the first place because they are very busy, and quite frankly, if there is an issue, they will probably wait until you have been here for almost a year (now, 2 years) and want us to get rid of you before you can make a claim against us.

But, if this does not happen, and we do not talk to you at all, then you are probably doing a really good job and we want to keep you, so just go with the thinking that no news is good news.

Just as I can remember my two best recruitment processes, I can remember my worst first day ever in a new organization, and without a doubt, it has overshadowed all of my first days anywhere.

I arrived early, I did not want to be late or risk issues with any traffic or transport delays, I would have been super-duper early, but I went for a coffee across the road first. On arrival, I checked in at reception, they had no idea who I was (not in a "don't you know who I am" kind of way, but a "welcome to the organization" kind of way would have been nice), and I asked for my manager.

The time when I had been asked to arrive came and went, and still, I remained at the same place. After another 10 minutes, I walked back to the desk, which was about 10 feet away from where I was, and got a, "Oh, I didn't realize you were still here, I'll e-mail again"—what a lovely welcome!

Another 15 minutes passed, and then, a member of the team came down to get me, or rather, they came to take me for coffee. After a few minutes, they shared that nobody was expecting me and that my manager was busy and would only see me for 10 minutes that day.

I had not got the date wrong; I checked several times. Does this happen to all new employees? This had to be rectified, for surely this cannot be normal practice. I learned that my manager had been told of my start date, but had forgotten to put it in her diary with all of the other (important) stuff she had to do. It took me 4 days to get a security pass because of a "form" that needed to be filled in and signed—by whom, I never discovered—almost 2 weeks to get IT access (another form), and 2 months before I sat in on the corporate induction, because we had to cancel the others as none of the managers who were scheduled to deliver some of the sessions could make it.

I do love a challenge (luckily), and I was not going to be disappointed by this as there was clearly a *lot* that needed to be improved, and this was just the induction period. What else would I find to get my teeth stuck into (I discovered very quickly, a lot).

I learned very quickly—on Day One, in fact, as I got to speak to all of my team, a lot of the employees, and several managers while I waited for everything to be set up—that while the people were willing, the processes were broken and nobody seemed able to simplify or fix the process. The majority of managers did not want anything radical or life-changing from the HR team; they just wanted the basics right, and seemingly, we could not do any of that either.

I joined the organization with over 40 outstanding ER issues and seven ongoing ETs (employment tribunals) among another HR team restructure processes—one had only just happened when I joined and I was the last appointment made, an organization-wide restructure and redundancy process, a high number of underperforming managers, and a leadership team that saw HR as a pure admin function that could not even administrate effectively. I left with one ET outstanding and 11 ER cases as a result of the organizational restructure, which saw many employees redundant at the end of the process.

The corporate induction was cringeworthy when I eventually got on it; a lot of the information was irrelevant, and the passion from most of the managers presenting was lacking so much, I could have fallen asleep under the desk.

My team had designed an amazing interactive induction process with visits to sites, different managers delivering different sessions, a shorter process with a local induction that managers would deliver themselves to ensure their teams knew what they needed to know, and the onboarding process involving facilities and IT, so that passes and IT access were sorted straightaway. And most importantly, all employees would receive a welcome letter from the CEO on the day they arrived.

The process was rejected because of time and cost restrictions despite the CEO saying the induction needed to be improved.

What a message!

"We want you to work here, but we don't think you need to know anything about us; you are here to do a job, so here's your desk, thanks for your time, we will pay you at the end of the month."

Of course, the first few months in a role are more than IT access and a corporate induction, but if these areas are lacking, what does it say about your organization as an employer? What does it say about your culture, the leadership, and how much you value your employees?

The "new and improved" induction that I mentioned earlier was not designed in isolation in the silo of the HR function. It had been designed with input from employees, new and existing, employee representatives, managers, and the HR team. And in one 10-minute discussion, it had been thrown out by the board, and we were told to just modify what we already had. We did get it approved eventually, but it should not have been so hard.

An employee's first few months in a role should involve supporting, nurturing, educating, growing, and training from the management with support from HR. A great few months pave the way for a great career with the organization, no matter how long our people stay. It should not be difficult.

So, why is it so hard?

First, regardless of the HR process for induction, managers need to understand their role. The HR element of induction is largely the administration and coordination of the process. Without managers and leaders engaging in the process and seeing the importance of it, whatever the shape and size of the packaging, the content will always be lacking. Because managers see it as an "HR thing," it is easy for them to pass the buck. AGILE HR is about everyone being an accountable adult.

Second, we focus on what we feel employees need to know about the organization, instead of focusing on what will help them embed into the organization.

The objective setting for the first few months should include things along the lines of spending time with a "buddy" or mentor, getting to know team members, meeting with some of the key stakeholders, understanding the customer journey, and so on. It is not purely about "hit £10k of sales," "learn IT system," and so on.

New employees should be met with regularly and made to feel as though they can approach their manager or appointed contact with what could be considered as the silliest of questions. I personally do not believe in silly questions. If you need to know something like how to make a coffee, or the best place for lunch, then you need to ask. These small things can make a big difference to how you settle in to the organization.

And why do we call it an induction period?

Induction *noun*

UK /ɪnˈdʌk.ʃən/ US /ɪnˈdʌk.ʃən/

noun

an occasion when someone is formally introduced into a new job or organisation, especially through a special ceremony:

Their induction into the church took place in June.
Her induction as councillor took place in the town hall.
An induction course/programme/ceremony.

There has been a lot of discussion over the last few years about whether it should be a "trial period," a "getting to know you period," a "test it out period." I do not see anything wrong with the word "induction"; everyone knows what it means, but rather than leaving new employees sitting in the reception for hours, and then, telling them they have been forgotten about and that they need to wait for weeks to get IT or security access, let us make it a ceremony, a celebration of them joining the business.

Let us find ways of removing or at least minimizing the vast amounts of rainforest that we send you prior to joining (which will be much more simple a task when our policies reflect that we treat people as adults), and give you what you need in a more interactive way (videos, podcasts, online learning, audiobooks), signing only the "must have paperwork," and then, let us find a way to minimize the fear on Day One, by inviting you to one of the greatest ceremonies you will ever attend. A ceremony where you are made to feel important, and valued, and respected, and where you get to know about the organization and all of the "silly" things that will help your journey start more easily and run more smoothly for you.

And then, let us pair you with a buddy/mentor to help support you even more, and let us encourage your manager to set you important and relevant objectives and have regular contact with you, and then, let us involve you in the design of the induction ceremony for the next round of new starters, because you will know what would have helped you settle in more.

How about that for an induction?

Before you read on, take some time, and consider your own induction process.

- Does it reflect your brand?
- Would it excite you as a potential candidate?
- If you could wave a magic wand and create the best recruitment process for your organization, what would you create?
- How could you then implement this in your organization?

Then, answer:

- Does this allow candidates to demonstrate their ability?
- Does this encourage ideas, creativity, and innovation from candidates?
- Does it reflect that your candidates are individuals?
- Does it demonstrate that your people are leaders?
- Does it demonstrate that the candidates have a shared purpose, a shared vision, and shared values, and would it be something that they would feel proud about sharing with their family and friends?

Take some time to answer these questions and share your thoughts with your team, your manager, or in the HR Hub.

4.3   Well-being

I have included this as a separate section as some of it does not fit into Reward, and yet, it is an important area to consider when creating practices and frameworks for your people.

Many of us strive for greater work–life balance—something I do not think we will ever really find, given the hours we work each week, and so, I prefer the term "life balance," but that is not always possible either.

The growing use of technology means we are accessible 24 hours a day, we are expected to work harder for longer to get the job done, and add to that, the normal everyday pressures of bills, family commitments, friends, and wanting to stay active—and we are already sinking.

When I was appointed to a new post, I was going through some reports for a board meeting late one night for a meeting the next day and my boss sent me an e-mail; I responded. She came straight back to me and told me not to answer at this time of night to anyone from work, including her, as once started, the expectation would be that I continued. She was right.

Over the last few years, I have been conscious about my own well-being, largely due to two operations, the ailments of which were related, I believe, largely to stress.

My morning routine now consists of yoga and meditation, with some added meditation, if required, throughout the day as well as running, cycling, and going to the gym. I journal at night to clear my head and do not touch (or very rarely) my phone or laptop after 8 p.m. at night so that I get a better night's sleep and wake up feeling refreshed in the morning. Lack of sleep is the biggest driver toward stress, depression, and anxiety, as we saw earlier on in the book.

And I have discovered that when I rest more, I am more productive. Even a walk at lunchtime can be beneficial, and yet, so many of us sit in meetings for 10 hours a day with little food, water, or air, and wonder why our energy and our mood are affected.

The concept of employee well-being has grown in popularity over the past few years, but is it something new or just a clever relabelling of traditional absence management, occupational health, and good management practice?

What programs and initiatives are taking place under this heading and how effective are they for both employee and employer?

Stress and other mental health conditions are now among the main causes of employee absence, according to the CIPD absence management survey (2006).

The Health and Safety Executive (HSE) estimates that stress costs businesses £3.8 billion a year.

The increase in obesity is also a major worry for policymakers. The Department of Health (DoH) research reveals that if current trends continue, the proportion of men who are obese will have risen to 33 percent from 22 percent in 2003. The number of obese women is set to rise from 23 percent to 28 percent over the same period.

Personal well-being does not exist on its own or in the workplace, but within a social context. Recent years have seen individuals' lives affected by social, lifestyle, and employment changes, but despite these shifts, people still have the same basic physical and mental needs for social support, physical safety, health, and a feeling they are able to cope with life. Increasingly, they are demanding that employers help them to achieve this, particularly as a large part of their lives are spent at work.

We define it as: creating an environment to promote a state of contentment, which allows an employee to flourish and achieve their full potential for the benefit of themselves and their organization. Well-being is more than an avoidance of becoming physically sick.

It represents a broader bio-psycho-social construct that includes physical, mental, and social health. Fit employees are physically and mentally able, willing to contribute in the workplace, and likely to be more engaged at work.

Well-being is a subjective experience. It can involve practical measures such as introducing healthy food or a gym at work, or perhaps less tangible initiatives, such as working to match the values and beliefs held by employees with those of their organization.

It could be argued that a change in the way employees are engaged in discussions about how their work is organized could have more of an impact on an individual's well-being than the introduction of a corporate gym.

Well-being will run the risk of being dismissed as a gimmick unless those involved in its introduction and promotion demonstrate the positive business benefits that it brings.

To be effective, employee well-being needs to be part of a regular business dialogue and has to be deeply embedded into an organizational culture. The well-being dialogue can be beneficial to employees.

Many organizations are trying to create a balance between maximizing productivity and the risk that their employees may burn out, making costly errors or resigning. An understanding of a holistic approach that underlies well-being, and development of initiatives, coordinated with other HR policies, can offer an approach to achieve that balance.

Organizational well-being is about many things, but some of the most important include employees having meaningful and challenging work and having an opportunity to apply their skills and knowledge in effective working relationships with colleagues and managers in a safe and healthy environment.

Well-being-orientated organizations provide the tools to get the job done and the opportunity to achieve personal aspirations while maintaining work–life (or life) balance.

Some of the essential factors leading to organizational and personal well-being are:

- values-based working environment and management style
- open communication and dialogue
- team-working and cooperation
- clarity and unity of purpose
- flexibility, discretion, and support for reasonable risk-taking
- a balance between work and personal life
- the ability to negotiate workload and work pace without fear of reprisals or punishment
- being fairly compensated in terms of salary and benefits

The employer also has a duty to ensure that its culture fosters a positive working environment. The need for social justice and human rights has been addressed in a CIPD statement on human rights (2007).

Employers should focus on creating a workplace culture in which everyone feels included, valued, and respected. To foster personal responsibility and engagement, a balanced approach is needed to address diverse stakeholder and organizational interests and preferences. Creating a climate of mutual respect and dignity will foster improved working relationships and contribute to productivity and business performance.

Perhaps the most important factor in employee well-being is the relationships employees have with their immediate manager. Where there are strong relationships between managers and staff, levels of well-being are enhanced. A good manager will recognize the strengths, likes, and dislikes of their team members (treating them as individuals), and will be able to recognize when the volume or complexity of the work is too much for a particular team member.

The more capable that line managers are in identifying the personal interests and concerns of the individual, the more likely they will be able to create a team where employee well-being becomes an integral part of getting the job done.

Employee well-being involves:

- maintaining a healthy body by making healthy choices about diet, exercise, and leisure
- developing an attitude of mind that enables the employee to have self-confidence, self-respect, and be emotionally resilient
- having a sense of purpose, feelings of fulfillment and meaning
- possessing an active mind that is alert, open to new experiences, curious, and creative
- having a network of relationships that are supportive and nurturing

Marks & Spencer is known nationally as an employer who values employees. Historically, well-being was delivered through a traditional benefits package, including flexible working and family-friendly policies.

In addition, a good physical working environment was provided, including good catering facilities.

Other ancillary benefits for some or all employees included hairdressing, chiropody, dentistry, massage, yoga, mindfulness, and other holistic services. As the business moved through a change management program, it was realized that more focus was needed on the health and well-being areas that were directly affected by the workplace.

The UK Government strategy for health and well-being and vocational rehabilitation were considerations for the HR and occupational health teams within Marks & Spencer, with management referrals to occupational health being predominantly for guidance on the management of individuals with a musculoskeletal health issue.

The decision was taken to trial a fast referral for physical therapy for those employees who have their personal and work life affected by such health issues, recognizing that the NHS process for assessment and treatment via the general practitioner was overburdened.

Fourteen stores were involved in a 3-month trial. All employees who were in the workplace and experiencing musculoskeletal problems were eligible for referral for physical therapy. Employees who contacted the store to advise them of absence owing to musculoskeletal health issues were also referred for physical therapy. The employee was provided with an appointment within 72 hours from referral. Referral for assessment and treatment were not dependent on the cause being workplace-specific.

The total number of employees participating in the trial was 4,000. Of this number, 192 (4.8 percent) were referred from 13 stores.

During the trial, employees who received treatment were able to continue in the workplace alongside their team members, employees who had experienced delays in accessing NHS treatment were appreciative of the service, and employees absent were able to return to work to undertake restricted workplace duties.

The 3-month trial demonstrated an 8 percent reduction in employee sickness absence for musculoskeletal health issues. Store management teams reported additional benefits: improved morale of the departmental team and the general store, all of which are difficult to estimate in financial terms, improved customer service, and improved efficiencies.

Take some time now to consider your own personal well-being, and then, the things you have in place for the people in your organization.

Personal well-being
- Do I make it a priority?
- At what times throughout the day does my energy slump?
- How can I counteract this? Solutions—Walking, less carbs/sugar/caffeine, more water, less back to meetings etc.
- What one change can I commit to for myself?
- How can I encourage my team to make their well-being a priority?
- Does the culture in my organization prioritize my well-being?

Organizational well-being
- Does it reflect your brand?
- Does it help you and motivate you as an employee?

- If you could wave a magic wand and create the best environment for employee well-being in your organization, what would you create?
- How could you then implement this in your organization?

Then, answer
- Does this allow employees to feel supported and able?
- Does this encourage ideas, creativity, and innovation for employees?
- Does it reflect that your people are individuals?
- Does it demonstrate that your people are leaders?
- Does it demonstrate that your people have a shared purpose, a shared vision, and shared values, and would it be something that they would feel proud about sharing with their family and friends?

Take some time to answer these questions and share your answers and reflections with your team and or your senior leaders.

4.4   Reward

For this section, as in the online program and the workshop, we will look at reward in its totality, so that includes salaries, bonuses, pay rises, benefits, and gifts.

I started my career with the John Lewis Partnership, first at Waitrose, and then, I transferred to John Lewis. My salary was great, not just for retail, but for anyone in their first role out of education. I got amazing discounts, subsidized lunch, and of course, the much-talked-about annual bonus, based on profit shares.

In addition to this, when you hit 25 years' service, you also receive 6 months paid leave, plus an annual pay rise based on your individual performance (although 1 year, I received two pay rises for hitting and exceeding my objectives as a trainee), and totally unbeknownst to me, if you had been given amazing feedback or helped a colleague, you could also go and select a gift, there and then, from the MD's gift cupboard.

Wow.

Now, depending on which data you look at, I am a millennial. I was born in 1980 and do indeed want autonomy and purpose, so when I was promoted, and then, told no positions would be available for the next 6 years (I was 24 at the time and was not going to be at the same level for the next 6 years), I left the John Lewis Partnership, somewhere I thought I would spend my entire career.

No amount of money in the world was going to keep me there. That said, throughout my life, there have been times when money has been the driver. I think it happens to us at differing times of our lives, but for me, with kids, and a mortgage, and a personal life I wanted to maintain, money, at times, has been my main driver.

At another of my employers, we would receive Easter Eggs every Easter, a £50 gift voucher every Christmas, an occasional annual bonus, a performance-related bonus, chocolates and ice cream at varying points of the year "just because," a letter from the CEO when we were recognized for doing a good job, a birthday card, awards for delivering the values, with our photo on the wall of fame and other ad hoc things throughout the year. Much of this, however, then became expected by staff and not seen as a reward of any kind. The enthusiasm from staff was lost, the want to reward staff was important to the CEO.

Reward, I fear, will always be the biggest bone of contention with our people, even though we know from the research that it is not seen as the biggest priority of what motivates us or engages us, but the good news is, it does not have to be this way.

But, we need to make a lot of changes first.

First, I believe we need to pay people what they are worth. Not what we pay everyone else on the same level or grade, but what the person is worth. What is the value for their expertise and experience? If someone comes to you with exactly what you need and more, why would you only pay the rate you pay every new starter? You dangle the carrot of the pay rise after "probation," and somehow think the annual bonus is enough to incentivize them. I do not know anyone that can explain to their employees how the bonus is calculated each year because it is usually hidden in some algorithm of a spreadsheet or other database.

Congratulations, you have worked really hard this year, so we take your grade and work out how much of the pot that will give you, and then, take your salary into consideration, and then, we use a percentage of the profits, although we do not know how much yet, and put that into a pot, and then, we mix it all up together and come up with a figure that will take us three or four months to pay you because it is so complicated, and then, let us hope you are not one of the unlucky ones that seems to have vanished from our spreadsheet, in which case, you will have to wait an extra month because it is too much work for Finance to pay you now. Same time, next year?

There is a lot of research on this topic and a lot of great work being done by a lot of companies to change the way we reward our people. I have attached some of these examples in the resource section, so I do not want to labor the point on this one too much, for you will never move onto the next section, but from my own experience, we need to:

- Pay great salaries and forget the bonus—It is often used as a carrot, but is usually a stick.
- Reward our employees with Thank You and handwritten notes, or Easter eggs and a visit to the cupboard of gifts to make a selection, something on the spot and unexpected—We all like a unexpected reward, it is good for a release of our happy hormones and makes us more productive.
- Be fair and consistent but lose the complicated frameworks, bureaucracy, and red tape—Have a framework, but not a cast iron policy that nobody has the key for.
- Introduce reward programs that allow your people to select what they want—gym membership, child care vouchers, extra holiday, increased pay. We all have different needs and wants, and this changes at different points in our life. Child care vouchers were great for me 10 years ago; what use are they to me now?

I was speaking to a new client just this week, who has moved from the private to the public sector, and she said what she finds most difficult is the fact that their employees talk about their *band* like it is a badge of honor. I'm an "A" band, and I'm a "E" band, and in reality, what most of this means is that they have been in the post for so long that their annual mandatory salary increase has moved them up and up and up, and that is all that will happen each year until they leave. How incentivizing is that?

Before you move on, take some time and consider how you reward your people.

- Does it reflect your brand?
- Would it excite you as a potential candidate?
- If you could wave a magic wand and create the best way to reward your people, what would you create?
- How could you then implement this in your organization?

Then, answer:

- Does this allow employees to feel their ability is recognized?
- Does this encourage ideas, creativity, and innovation for candidates?
- Does it reflect that your employees are individuals?
- Does it demonstrate that your people are leaders?
- Does it demonstrate that your employees have a shared purpose, a shared vision, and shared values, and would it be something that they would feel proud about sharing with their family and friends?

Take some time to answer these questions and share them with your team or your managers.

4.5   Learning and Development

I left school immediately after my A levels and started my career in retail management. I now hold two degrees, countless other qualifications and certificates, and skills and experience, and am currently completing my PhD.

I love learning, and over the years, I have spent thousands of pounds and hours on my own personal and professional development. I look at what I want to learn, or where I want to develop further, and I find a way to do it. Sometimes, it is as simple as reading a book; sometimes, an online course; sometimes, a program; sometimes, a degree—it depends on what I want to get from it and how I think it will add value to me, my life, and my work.

Yet, we do not very often look at the different ways or different learning that our people want and need. I have worked for employers where we have spent months collating skills and training audits only for the information to be irrelevant when we actually started designing the programs. And don't get me started on how much money is wasted on trainers and venues to have nobody show up to a course, when everyone has been sent them 20 different reminders (even copying in their managers)—how very adult of us.

When my MD at Chrysalis suggested we start delivering e-learning, I was totally against it. Having been involved in e-learning since the late 1990s, as a participant, and then, as a purchaser (because it is what my employers wanted), it was not engaging, I never learned anything, and I certainly did not embed any of the learning in the workplace. I did, however, get to put the stats onto my database to say how many people we had trained and how much we had saved on last year—pat on the back for me, yay!

But at Chrysalis Consulting, we researched, and we found a system that I liked, and a way of designing learning that was fun, engaging, and allowed you time to embed the learning and keep on learning after the course was finished.

We do this in different styles for our clients, with a very different feel—for some clients, it is a simple resource library; for others, it is a MOOC, a long program; and for others, it compliments and works with their face-to-face material.

Research tells us we learn best when it is social and when we can embed the learning immediately. How many times have you been on a course and promised yourself you will make all of the changes as soon as you get back to the office, only to be swamped the minute you step back in, and never get round to doing any of the stuff you intended to.

Research also tells us that it can take us 60 days before we learn to make a change—not the previously thought 12 days—and up to 11 times of practice before we learn something new, and yet, much of our learning is structured in a way where you sit through death by PowerPoint all day, fill in a workbook, and then voilà, you are ready to be awesome.

In the resources section, you will find our infographic that highlights some of the stats about learning effectiveness. It shows that we lose 80 percent of what we learn in the first 9 days, 80 percent!

It also shows that only 5 percent is learned from what we see and hear, while 90 percent is learned when we teach others and when we put the learning into immediate application.

Instead, though, of investing our time in on-the-job training, mentoring, or sponsorship, we spend hundreds of thousands a year on external training that does not take into account any of the learning effectiveness requirements, and of course, then when money is tight, the training budget is the first thing to go and we stop learning altogether.

At the very beginning of this book, I said my advice was to go through it once, and then, dip in and out when needed.

That is what I believe we need to provide for our people. A time and a place when they can grab and go, where they can get what they need when they need it, and if something is missing, we will create it for them or support them in finding it for themselves.

When you need to learn something new, where do you usually go?

For me and most of my family and friends, it is Google, without a doubt, and I always find what I need, even if it involves three Youtube videos before I get the full picture.

The world of technology and learning is no longer just something that happens in a classroom or on a training course. We are surrounded by, and, in some cases, overloaded by data and information and learning.

I have just tallied up the amount of learning opportunities that I was sent by e-mail last week—64.

Sixty four! Seven invitations to workshops, 14 webinar invitations, and 43 online courses. I have not said yes to any of them; if I had accepted them all, then I would have no time to get any of the learning completed or embedded, and given that we lose 80 percent of the learning in 9 days if we do not embed it, most of what I learned would be forgotten, and therefore, a waste of time and money.

We do this a lot when it comes to developing our employees. Instead of giving them access to learning or supporting their requests to learn what they need when they need it, we plough endless resources into designing programs and courses that we make mandatory for all employees, and tell them there will be consequences if they do not attend, and then, at the end of the year, we wonder why performance of the individual and the team and the organization has not improved.

It is not rocket science.

I include coaching in this section as well.

Coaching is great. I say this as a coach and someone who still works with a coach. And while the session may allow for moments of clarity and understanding, the change can only really occur if time is put aside to make the changes and act on the changes.

I also suggest that clients allow at least an hour for self-reflection and planning at the end of the coaching session and advise that the sessions take place outside of the place of work. There is nothing worse than leaving a session or even a meeting and feeling pumped up and ready to make a change only for the opportunity to be lost because you got back to your desk and became swamped with the day-to-day tasks and never got around to implementing what you wanted to do.

This happens continuously with learning in the workplace, and we need to find a new way of allowing people to learn what they need to learn when they need to learn it to allow them chance to implement it, action it, and continue to improve.

Consider now how you train and develop your people.

- Does it reflect your brand?
- Would it excite you as a potential candidate?
- If you could wave a magic wand and create the best way for your people to learn, what would you create?
- How could you then implement this in your organization?

Then answer:

- Does this allow employees to feel their ability is recognized?
- Does this encourage ideas, creativity, and innovation for candidates?
- Does it reflect that your employees are individuals?
- Does it demonstrate that your people are leaders?
- Does it demonstrate that your employees have a shared purpose, a shared vision, and shared values, and would it be something that they would feel proud about sharing with their family and friends?

Take some time to answer these questions, and then, share your learning with your team and or your manager before moving on.

4.6   Performance Management

I am really looking forward to my performance review, said no one ever.

I cannot ever remember sitting in a performance review meeting with any of my managers that felt engaging and inspiring. They were always more of a conversation that focused on a run-up to the grade I would receive while we went through the form, and then, discussed my objectives for the next year and what training I wanted and needed.

The best feedback, support, and encouragement were the ad hoc feedback I received throughout the year, and usually in a more informal discussion.

And how many times has your HR team been bombarded with requests for the previous year's form so that employees and managers can review what they wrote and what the objectives were?

Annual appraisals happen annually (the clue is in the name). While I was at John Lewis, this related to the anniversary of your start date, but for many organizations, it is a companywide annual event, with all staff being met with at the same time of year.

And yet still, when the time comes around, managers and senior managers will ask for extra time to complete them because they do not have the time, and in many cases, you go back to them with a No, because this will delay the payment to their employees—how wonderful!

I focus mainly on annual performance reviews here, but of course, this also includes probation reviews and at any point when you are formally or informally focusing on the performance of your people.

Back in 2009, I designed a rolling appraisal process for my organization; it was not without its faults, but it did mean that conversations were happening more often, objectives were more relevant, and performance increased, and I have introduced it for a number of clients since.

But the biggest issue relates to the grade, and usually because the grade carries a price with it associated with an annual bonus, and if you were an "A" last year, you better be an "A" this year because you have already booked your holiday or spent the bonus in some other way before it is even in the bank.

Then, when the tick box exercise (the form itself) is completed, you send the form off, there is a meeting to moderate the grades at which point your grade could change, depending on how many people have been awarded the same grade, a bit of a bun fight happens, and then, payments are made.

I have never been fan of forced distribution, not one bit, but still we do it, because we were taught in the 1980s that bell curves were the best thing since sliced bread, and if we do not do annual reviews, what will we replace them with?

For 2 years in a row, I was on a moderation panel where it was evident that managers were not managing their people effectively, nor giving them constructive, helpful, or motivating feedback.

The biggest offender reported directly to the CEO. I gave my feedback on him and how he was managing the process directly to him, and then, to the CEO, and yet, still no change.

The offender's team had the highest rate of sickness absence and performance issues than any other department, and had more complaints from customers than any other team, yet they were all awarded As.

The panel downgraded them each year, only for the CEO to put them back up again. The second year, we had moved to rolling reviews, where a grade was awarded each quarter and averaged over the year. The offender had created the calculations and despite a few Bs throughout the year, they still ended up with all As by the time of the final assessment.

This was a big issue, and in the third year, I finally won my argument with him and the CEO, but why had this been allowed to happen for so long?

What we need are relevant objectives, more frequent feedback, and to take pay out of the equation altogether. I know companies that have scrapped reviews altogether, some with success, others not so, and where it did not work was where managers were still underperforming, did not give any feedback other than when something went wrong, and their teams felt demotivated and began to disengage, and where a learning culture was a myth and not something that was played out in reality.

And unfortunately, it is these managers that we create such tight measures for when it comes to managing the performance of our employees. But in reality, the process is worthless if the people are incapable of making it work. And really, this is the same for any process or policy that we implement.

A piece of paper outlining a process is only as good as the people that action the process.

If performance management is an issue for your organization, take some time and work out how much the annual reviews are costing you each year—not so much in terms of bonus, although you can add that later, but in time taken to prepare, complete, write up, send off, moderate, process payments and issue letters.

Take that figure, work out how it could be better spent, and submit a proposal to change it or stop it all together, but do find a framework or something else to ensure that employees are set objectives and are able to have meaningful and helpful conversations with their managers, even if it is over a coffee every month.

I am sure you could fund a lot of coffee and cake with the amount you will find.

This, just as reward, is probably an area where you may be faced with a LOT of challenge from the business. Because this process is all we know, and it is what the management schools tell us we need, and we will think we need to replace it with something else. Do not create another process; find a productive way to provide feedback that engages and motivates your people and improves performance.

Find a way to set clear objectives and have better conversations with your people inside and outside of a formal review process.

Consider now how you manage the performance of your people.

- Does it reflect your brand?
- Would it excite you as a potential candidate?
- If you could wave a magic wand and create the best way for your people to manage performance and provide feedback, what would you create?
- How could you then implement this in your organization?

Then, answer:

- Does this allow employees to feel their abilities are recognized?
- Does this encourage ideas, creativity, and innovation for candidates?
- Does it reflect that your employees are individuals?
- Does it demonstrate that your people are leaders?
- Does it demonstrate that your employees have a shared purpose, a shared vision, and shared values, and would it be something that they would feel proud about sharing with their family and friends?

Take some time to answer these questions in the workbook, your journal, or share your answers and reflections in the group.

4.7 Talent Management

How many times do we ask our people to think outside of the box when we want them to find solutions and new ideas, and yet, what do we do with them when it comes to talent? We put them in a box. A beautiful, carefully crafted nine-box grid or four-box grid where we have carefully considered what to label each box for fear of upsetting someone and we sit around a table and place their names in box.

What if there was no box?

I love the concept that we should act, think, and work like there was no box; how liberating that would be, to know there are no boundaries and that we can grow and stretch and flex in any way we can?

Why don't we think like that with our people and how often do we assign them a box without talking to them at all, but based on our own perception?

We make assumptions due to the length of service or performance ratings that people will automatically want to climb the corporate ladder, and yet, that is not always the case, and likewise, sometimes, we assume that someone is happy in a role, and so, we leave them there, plodding along until the day they leave or retire.

The John Lewis Partnership are great at having conversations about career aspirations and many of their roles are advertised internally so that you can move sideways, upwards, or downwards into a role that will give you what you want; it is great, and it also means that people will stay for longer because they get the variety and development they want and need.

Over the years, though, I have had discussions with people about needing to look externally for talent because we have "none" in the business.

How do we know if we do not look or ask?

New blood has its advantages, but so does home-grown talent. and just because there may not be anyone suitable in your team, it does not mean there aren't a dozen people that could do the job elsewhere in the business.

We do not always want to share, though, do we?

We want to keep our own people to ourselves, and in some cases, we do not want to promote our own team members because they do their role so well and we feel we will be lost without them.

Well, guess what?

If we do not nurture and develop those who are seeking to grow, they will leave anyway, and if at the point that they resign, you then decide to offer them a promotion or a pay rise, they may stay for a while, but when the emotional contract is broken, it is broken and there is rarely any going back.

John Lewis were great for growing and developing talent, and in fact, when I was promoted, I was promoted knowing I may need to wait for a role to come up.

Many people also believe that you can only move upward. If you take a sideways move or a step back, you must be some kind of failure or perhaps your performance is just not up to scratch. Our thinking and our approach to Talent Management is currently very linear, and as we talked about earlier, full of boxes.

But life is not like that, so why do we manage our talent like this?

What if you progressed through your career, and then, at the time that you had children (and this is for the mums and dads), you wanted a little less responsibility for a while, or less hours, and then, in a few years you wanted to move sideways to gain some new experience, and then, you wanted to move upward, and then, when your kids go off to university, you decide you do not want quite the senior role you had anymore because you are more financially secure and you want to take more holidays, or go to evening classes, or start a new hobby, or start dating your spouse again?

Or, if you are caring for elderly or sick relatives and you want to take your foot off the brakes a bit and be able to move into positions as they arise, whether it be up, down, or sideways.

Or, what if, you just want a slower pace, or less management, or less report writing, and you just want to enjoy your role?

Some people thought I was mad when I recruited an MD for the company I founded, but it works for me, and I like it. I love coaching and delivering workshops and working with clients and sitting in the office all day looking at accounts, marketing and all of the other administrative tasks that come with running a business do not make the most of my strengths. So, I recruited someone into the business who is great at creating and implementing processes and growing the business, and it allows me to focus more on not only what I love doing, but what I am good at.

And we should not be afraid of taking steps like this if it makes the most of our strengths and ensures that we love doing what we do.

I spent the first 18 years of my career climbing the corporate ladder, always chasing my next promotion and my next role and looking for the next project to help my teams continue to develop themselves and their skills. And I reached the top, and wondered what I was going to do for the rest of my working life. The more senior I had become, the more time I was spending creating strategies and managing the politics of the board and less time doing what I loved.

So, when I started Chrysalis Consulting, I knew I could go back to doing what I loved. Except that I could not. Several people had told me that when you run your own business, a large proportion of my time would be spent building the business instead of delivering the work and I could not see how that could be the case. But it was. There is so much to do and I just wanted to help clients.

I did not take the decision to recruit someone into the business lightly. I considered recruiting some admin support, but I would still need to manage this, and actually, while I love developing people, I did not want to manage anyone. I wanted to work with clients and create content without the responsibility of managing people. I had been doing that for years and I wanted a change. And some people find this weird. Why would I start a business and recruit someone else to run it?

Because after climbing as high as I wanted in the corporate world, I want to go back to my roots and do what I am good at. This may change, it may not, but having the choice and the freedom to do what I love doing keeps me passionate about the work I do, and away from the Monday-to-Friday syndrome that so many people experience on a weekly basis.

One of my previous employers had a customer service advisor who had been in her post for over 20 years; she had survived the mergers and was without a doubt the nicest advisor ever, and if you heard her on the phone with customers, or talking to and helping other team members, you could not fault her. If you could clone her, we would have no problem with customer service at all, ever, but she did not want to be a supervisor, or a manager and while she was happy to buddy up with new starters, she did not want to take them all. After all, how could she deliver great customer service if she was always training other people? She was talented, but did not want to move. She was happy to learn and picked up new systems and new ways of working brilliantly, but she did not want to move up the ladder, yet every year, her manager would tick the box as someone we should invest in and look to promote.

We should not be afraid of having conversations about how long someone thinks they will be in a role or stay in a company, and we should not penalize them if they do not see themselves being here forever. There is no such thing as a job for life anymore. Some people like variety and some people do not; some people want to develop and some people do not; some people want to learn new skills and some people do not. And we should not make the mistake of thinking that our talented people are those we should automatically look to promote by placing their name in a box.

I think it is great that a lot of organizations are now implementing career coaching into their talent and performance management thinking. It works. And this is not led by the manager with their employee, but with trained coaches from across the organization, who, through the coaching program, discuss the aspirations, challenges, and work of the coachee to help them grow in their role, and if they choose, to help them develop in preparation for their next career move, whether this be moving upward, sideways, or downward.

Organizations and the people within them are changing. New ways of working, new technology, new markets, mergers and acquisitions all provide a lot of opportunity to develop new skills, or utilize existing skills in a new way. Employees want more from their employers than a salary and a promotion, and we need to embrace this.

Boxes and grids no longer fit the needs of the people in the business, and yet, they are still seen as a useful business tool.

The only way we can genuinely manage our talent is through having better more informed conversations with our people, understanding what they really want and need, and then, supporting them as opportunities arise.

Consider now how you manage the talent in your organization.

- Does it reflect your brand?
- Would it excite you as a potential candidate?
- If you could wave a magic wand and create the best way for your people to manage performance and provide feedback, what would you create?
- How could you then implement this in your organization?

Then answer:

- Does it allow employees to develop in their abilities and have these recognized?
- Does it encourage ideas, creativity, and innovation for employees?
- Does it reflect that your employees are individuals?
- Does it demonstrate that your people are leaders?
- Does it demonstrate that your employees have a shared purpose, a shared vision, and shared values, and would it be something that they would feel proud about sharing with their family and friends?

Take some time to answer these questions and share your reflections with your team and or your senior leaders.

4.8   Leadership Development

When I was in second year sixth form, the general election was being held and our teachers wanted us to understand politics more by running our own campaigns, based on the political parties, their manifestos. and their promises and see who could create and run the best campaign and secure the most votes.

Our entire year group was responsible for researching the parties we had to represent, creating our own manifesto that was relevant to the school based on the manifestos created by the parties, presenting our manifesto to other year groups in the school, and then secure votes.

There were four political parties—The Conservatives, Labour, The Liberal Democrats, and The Monster Raving Loony Party. Each group was given a party to represent and I was selected to be the leader of The Liberal Democrats and people voted to work for me on the campaign. I did not see myself as a leader at that point, especially as the introvert that I am, but my team did, and so, for that one year, I became the leader of a political party. We came second when the votes were counted, losing only a few votes to The Raving Loonies, who were the two most good-looking and popular boys in the school.

How did that happen? It is not like school votes become a popularity contest, is it?

As a team, we reviewed our manifesto and did all we could to make the content simple and relevant for students in the school. I spoke with conviction at each of the year group assemblies throughout the school about how we would help them and also asked them what they wanted and needed to make school better for them. We could not deliver on all that was asked of us and we made no promises that we would not be able to keep. We were honest, and my team, who had self-selected themselves to run our campaign, was passionate, supportive, and delivered.

Now, this is not a story of politics, but for an area that was mostly a Labour constituency with a few Conservatives in place, I doubt that many parents would have been happy with their children voting Lib Dem. But we came second—by asking questions, listening, being honest, having passion, and speaking with passion and conviction.

We took it as a win as we certainly were not the Raving Loonies that many of the students would have voted for.

Leaders can shine, often in the most unlikely situations and are not always the people we think they are. They are not always the most popular, the most liked, or in the most senior positions, and yet, many of our promotions and leadership development programs are focused on a one-size-fits-all approach, where to lead, you must be an extrovert, be great at all aspects of leadership, and in a lot of cases, be the best person at the job and possibly also have the longest length of service.

It does not work like that.

One size does not fit all. I have never heard anyone praise the leadership development program for any improvements in the team, and yet, we spend thousands upon thousands on leadership development every year.

I was asked to pitch for a leadership development program with a potential client last year. I knew as soon as I walked into the room with the HR Director and the CEO that I was not going to win this pitch.

The CEO looked at me as I entered, briefly, rolled her eyes and spent most of our meeting looking at her notebook before asking me what I could offer to her senior managers who spend most of their time glued to their phones in meetings, and will do so if ever they get bored in a meeting, especially when they had more MBAs, degrees and even a higher level of coaching experience than me.

This is often a typical situation. We assume that because we gain letters after our names or complete a qualification that we know it all, but if they were all that good, and if the programs they had been on at some of the most prestigious business schools in the UK had provided any value, they would not need me, or anyone like me to help them work together as a team or to stop them using their phones in meetings. This is down to leadership, pure and simple.

We also fail to look at, or give opportunity for learning to be embedded once a course or program has been completed.

In Simon Sinek's book *Leaders Eat Last*, he states that "educational institutions and training programs today are focused not on developing great leaders but on training effective managers," and I tend to agree with him. Much of what we talk about and implement in our organizations when it comes to leadership development is, in fact, teaching effective management skills.

I was working with a team of directors delivering our LEADing The Way Programme and the finance director mentioned that he had tried engaging his team more in team meetings, but that he struggled to keep their attention and gain buy-in to the new initiatives he was trying to introduce. We explored how he was trying to engage his team at these meetings and he proudly spoke about his beautifully crafted PowerPoint presentations that were filled with important data and statistics about the business and how he wanted to build a more effective team who were able to engage better with their customers across the business.

I asked what was the most engaging meeting/presentation and what made it so. He talked about a seminar he had attended in London where the speaker had told story after story and made these stories relevant to the data he was presenting on quite a boring topic to help engage the audience. Was he telling stories to his team? No.

But this type of presentation was all he had ever been taught and he did not know how to change. We explored some options and at the nest meeting, he designed a shorter presentation (his comfort blanket) and had considered some stories to tell. He later informed me that as he started to work through his presentation, he stopped, turned the screen off and told stories and asked for opinions from his team. The best meeting ever, and he has grown from strength to strength ever since, with his team engaging more with their customers and performance improving.

In her book *Executive Presence*, Sylvia Ann Hewlett talks about leaders needing to demonstrate Executive Presence and states that this rests on three pillars: How you act (gravitas), How you speak (communication), and How you look (appearance). She goes on to say that we need to be focusing on all three of these areas, but that we should not try and do all of them if they are not our natural tendency. How is that for choice! And yet, we spend all of our time trying to box people into competency frameworks and roll out the same style of boring, ineffective training that we never embed into the business because we expect that as soon as our leaders have been given the information, they will be immediately changed.

Do a search on Google about what employees really want from their leaders and you will be overwhelmed with responses, but the most common traits listed are:

- A leader that encourages improvement
- A leader that gives praise and recognition
- A leader that recognizes improvement
- A leader that acknowledges their own shortfalls before criticizing others
- A leader that allow employees to save face and learn from their own mistakes
- A leader that is honest
- A leader that is fair
- A leader that is dependable
- A leader that encourages collaboration, and
- A leader that is responsive.

When did your programs ever include content that included any of this?

Search for leadership development training, and again, you will be swamped by the results, many of which focus on leadership skills and include:

- Presentation Skills
- Influencing and Networking
- Personal Brand
- Strategic Thinking and Planning
- Accountability
- Communication
- Difficult Conversations

Hundreds, if not thousands, of leadership training providers who deliver programs and courses focus on effective management skills, but not skills that create great leaders and certainly not anything that creates leaders who will meet the criteria of what employees want by the end of the program.

And if we think back to the masculine and feminine leadership traits that we discussed earlier in the book (page 14), then what our people want aligns more to the feminine than the masculine leadership traits, yet so many leadership and management programs focus on the masculine trait of "doing."

Admittedly, a Google search does not amount to a great deal of research into this area, but the key is to find out what your people want from their leaders, identify what the business needs from its leaders, and provide learning opportunities to meet the needs of your individual leaders that fills the gap.

When I was creating our LEADing The Way program, I did so in collaboration with some of our past and present clients, looked at the research, spoke to a number of different universities and employers, and created a solution that met these needs. There is a blend of group and 1-2-1 work and it looks at leadership, rather than management skills, but not everyone will want to do the program, and we will not accept everyone onto it that does.

Why?

Because if the learner is not committed to it, and they do not have the time, or the resource, or the passion to implement the changes, then it is a waste of their time and money.

I have always been deeply invested in my own personal and professional development and when I have had my mind set on learning something, I have been committed to doing it, whether my organization would pay for it or not, and since starting my own consultancy, I have invested thousands and thousands of pounds in ensuring I know what I need to know and I do what I need to do to learn it.

I have also discovered that trying to develop my weaknesses (I hate that word), my less strong areas, is a waste of time. I have learned that by developing my strengths further and surrounding myself with people who can do what I cannot, or who know what I do not, is best all round for everyone.

That is one of the reasons I recruited an MD to manage my company. I love working with clients, designing courses, writing books, helping others to grow and change. I do not like process, and quite frankly, I am no good at running a business, but I can lead, and motivate, and empower and I have a big vision and big ideas. Strategy, I can do; detail, I cannot.

Leadership development does not tend to focus on developing strengths even more, though, does it? It tries to squeeze leaders into a leadership box, where everyone has the same level of competency as everyone else and where everyone fits the same mold.

One of my previous CEOs was a total introvert, and when he presented, he would stand at the side of his PowerPoint, in the dark if he could, and speak to the room, but with no passion, energy, or enthusiasm, and the room would switch off, whereas another of my CEOs, also an introvert had so much energy, and passion, and enthusiasm that you felt energized and inspired each time he spoke.

As an introvert myself, I understand that these differences were about much more than presentation skills. The only difference between these two people was the ability to engage their people. The one introvert would hide in his office and not even acknowledge his people in the mornings or at any point throughout the day, whereas the other would walk the floor every day, talk to people, learn about them and their lives and families, and create relationships with all his staff.

Which one would you rather work with?

We have to stop assuming that a one-size-fits-all approach is what our leaders want and what our business needs. We need to understand our leaders, what their strengths are, and support them in developing more of that.

Let us not think outside the box; let us work like there isn't one.

Before you move on, consider the following:

- Does your leadership development program reflect the needs of your leaders and your people?
- Would it excite you as a participant?
- If you could wave a magic wand and create the best way for your leaders to develop, what would it be?
- How could you then implement this in your organization?

Then, answer:

- Does this allow candidates to demonstrate their ability?
- Does this encourage ideas, creativity, and innovation for candidates?

- Does it reflect that your candidates are individuals?
- Does it demonstrate that your people are leaders?
- Does it demonstrate that the candidates have a shared purpose, a shared vision, and shared values, and would it be something that they would feel proud about sharing with their family and friends?

Take some time to answer these questions and share your reflections with your team, your leaders, and in the HR Hub online community.

4.9   Employee Engagement and Communications

So many organizations, when you speak to them about employee engagement, see it as little more than a communications plan and how we provide messages to our people, rather than what will engage them.

Employee Engagement is about much more than communicating and it is also not about creating happy employees.

Happy employees may be completely disengaged from the organization. Some people are very motivated by security and unemployment. These people may be very content to fog the mirror. While these folks may not appear engaged, misinformed managers might not understand the difference between engaged employees, happy employees, and employees who are just happy to have a salary each month.

"Engaged employees are happy employees," someone recently had the misfortune of saying in front of me at a meeting. Why does this seemingly harmless statement frustrate me so much?

Because it is not true.

Even when you get a great 360-degree performance review, even when the engagement scores for your organization are through the roof, even when you have the most engaged workforce in your space (and you have lots of "Best Place to Work" lists and awards to prove it), your employees might still not be happy.

Engaged employees are far more likely to become disengaged if employers only think about making them happy. Instead of offering additional learning and development opportunities, for example, employers might focus on increasing bonuses, thinking that a happy employee is an engaged employee. To an engaged employee, this might be a nice one-time bump in pay. But it will not compensate for their investment in the organization in the way removing obstacles from their pet project just might. And we know from the research that money is not the biggest factor when it comes to motivating our people.

When we are engaged at work, we perform better, work better with others, and want to learn more (remember the 3Ps from the How the Brain Works chapter—Positive Actions, Positive Interactions, and Positive Thoughts), and when we are engaged, so too are our customers, yet sometimes, we seek to overcomplicate things.

And as with most of what we do, we create a survey to find out how engaged people are, and then, create initiatives or strategies around what we need to improve. When I started at one company, a list of 164 things (yes, you read that right, 164) came out of the engagement survey and there had been six meetings—yes, six—before I joined to see how many of the 164 things we would prioritize.

Err, a maximum of three.

Anymore than three at a time and we would not achieve anything. "But we need to do them," I was told, "We have to report back to staff in 3 months on how we have done with them all."

So, a year after a survey of carefully selected questions had been pulled together, and the survey had been delayed three times because of redundancies, audits, or new managers, six meetings and 164 objectives, and we were going to deliver them all because we needed to go back to staff, we were still discussing the priorities—ludicrous.

And then, on top of all of this, we wanted to start pulse surveys once a month to gather feedback form employees so that they could tell us how we were doing. I do not think it would need rocket science to find the answer to this one. Let me guess—yep, the same as last month: no change and no progress.

With one employer and with many of my clients, instead of surveys, we facilitate engagement workshops. Nothing fancy, just me in a room with a flipchart and some tea and coffee, asking questions of no more than 15 employees at a time, of varying lengths of service and across different levels and from different roles. Some of the typical questions include:

- What attracted you to apply for a job here?
- Why did you accept?
- Do we deliver what we said we would?
- Why have you stayed?
- What do you love most?
- What frustrates you?
- What would you improve?

More valuable feedback has been received from these sessions than from any survey that employees have previously completed and employees felt heard and valued and the organization was able to take the comments and feedback from these sessions and quickly initiate changes. The organization was making a difference, not discussing what was a priority and getting nowhere.

The suggestions from each of these sessions varied; one person suggested a map of the floors or even some sort of sign to say which department was where, more difficult with hot-desking or agile working, but they said this would help new employees find their way and it did—lampposts were put in place. Another employee suggested every new starter have a buddy—a buddy system was put in place. Many suggested that IT, Facilities, and HR work together more effectively. And there were, of course, lots of conversation about the heating in the office, which we never did resolve.

Some of the most helpful was about change needing to be implemented more quickly and effectively, more analysis of the external markets, and less internal navel-gazing, people wanting to be thanked when they had done a good job, being able to spend more time with their manager, and seeing a more visible leadership team.

The visible leadership team suggestion did not quite go to plan, they just rotated their meetings to other offices, so we broke it down further, and said visible and engaging leadership, less meetings, more floor walking, and talking. It helped. This sort of change would have taken years to implement if we were waiting on another survey outcome.

At another employer of mine, to help employees understand more of what the leadership team experienced and had to deal with on a regular basis, a board game was created and used as a team game at our staff conference. Everyone was split into teams and we were allocated roles on the team, a board game, and some money; it was bit like monopoly.

We would roll the dice and take our turns, and on some spaces, would lose or gain money or people and have to carry on regardless, as there was a business to run. Every so often, an announcement would be made over the tannoy with bad news from the regulator, or a poor audit outcome, or a change to a legal framework or policy, and changes would have to be made.

The team with the most money at the end of the game won, but only if they had all of their key people in place and a high engagement score. The game was simplistic, it was a bit of fun, and by the end of it, the employees understood much more about the complexities of the business and what their manager had to deal with daily, and why change needed to be implemented.

Your most engaged employees might irritate you a little bit. They may propose wild ideas, get frustrated when projects are derailed, and volunteer for everything. They may rarely seem super happy, because they are busy pushing the envelope. These are people you want in your organization. In fact, you want their lack of appreciation for the status quo to infect those around them.

Stop perpetuating the myth that happy = engaged. You do not need to sacrifice one for the other, but stop creating an equivalency between the two. Tell your managers and your employees that while you think their happiness (and their well-being for that matter) is important, their engagement is crucial. Listen when they tell you how to help them become more engaged and act; do not wait 12 months and take no action at all.

The qualities that make each workforce engaged are going to be totally unique. Zappos has worked hard to create a distinct and engaged workforce. You know what else leader Tony Hsieh has done? He has tried to revitalize the downtown Las Vegas area. His stamp is on that project as much as it is on the way he structured the Zappos workforce. Importing programs from some other industry or business will not make your employees happy or engaged.

Focus on changing attitudes, not communications plans or programs. When faced with poor results, many executives change the program instead of the attitude. Instead of swapping out one useless campaign for another, take the time to talk to your employees before selecting a new option to increase engagement. You might be surprised at what you find out.

Before you move on, consider the following;

- Does your employee engagement reflect the needs of your leaders and your people?
- Would it excite you as a potential employee?
- If you could wave a magic wand and create the best way for your people to be engaged, what would it be?
- How could you then implement this in your organization?

Then answer:

- Does this allow your people to demonstrate their ability?
- Does it encourage ideas, creativity, and innovation for employees?
- Does it reflect that your people are individuals?
- Does it demonstrate that your people are leaders?
- Does it demonstrate that your people have a shared purpose, a shared vision, and shared values, and would it be something that they would feel proud about sharing with their family and friends?

Take some time to answer these questions and share your responses with your team and senior leaders, or better still, arrange a session or two to talk to your employees using some of the questions I mentioned earlier on in the chapter and compare the outcomes from this to your latest survey, and then, share your findings with the business.

4.10   Exit

When it comes to employees who are leaving your business, the end of this journey does not have to mean the end of their journey with you completely. Yet, we prefer to break all ties with our people when they tell us they are leaving or we have to tell them it is time to go, and we just want to ensure that we get all of our property and equipment back.

The statistics are out there to say that most employees leave because of their manager, although with most people only now staying in jobs for 2 or 3 years, it is sometimes just because they want to try something new and because of our linear talent management programs, we are not to meet the requirements of our people.

There are, of course, a number of ways people leave—they resign, are dismissed for conduct or performance issues, or are made redundant. It is how we treat our employees at each of these stages that makes a difference, though. And as we talked about in the recruitment section of this book, with more and more people watching us online, any negative comments or feedback can significantly impact our brand and our reputation.

People may resign for a plethora of reasons—from personal matters, to development opportunities, to relocating, pay, starting their own business, or something else. How we treat them matters.

At one of my employers, a member of the HR team was relocating due to her husband's new job, she had been heavily involved with the implementation of a new system and she worked from her new home for us until the system was finished, and then, found a new job in her new city. She stayed in contact for years.

We make it difficult, though, in a lot of cases. We do not let people leave early because we are paying them or they won't have given enough notice, so we hold them to ransom and make them work for as long as we possibly can.

In some cases, we prevent exiting employees from having access to any of our systems but still expect them to show up every day, and do what exactly? And for some, we just stop including them because we believe they have shown us no loyalty.

Very AGILE!

Some companies welcome their leavers back with open arms, and why shouldn't you? If they loved us once, they know what we are about and if their reason was nothing to do with anything we had done, why wouldn't we have them back?

Some companies offer Refer a Friend schemes; you are not going to let your friends down, after all, and some encourage their people to keep in contact with them, even offering some freelance or project work.

Yet, for the majority, it is a resignation acknowledgement letter saying how much we owe them or vice versa, a list of all of the things they need to return, and an exit interview form that you will probably never return, because the exit interview process is usually flawed.

Of course, if you are dismissing your people for anything other than redundancy, then a more formal approach may be the right way to go about it, but not for every circumstance.

Years ago, at the end of a redundancy process, my team and I were brought flowers and chocolates along with Thank You cards, from exiting employees.

Why?

We had followed the process, it is a legal requirement, but we had treated them as people at every stage of the process, keeping them updated, providing a safe space for them to come and talk about their issues and concerns, helped with CV and interview preparation, and even contacting employers in the local area who did similar work to us and working with the other company to design some assessment centers. Some of them, we were able to find jobs for; others were able to do this on their own; some went self-employed; and some returned years later, when we had new roles come up.

Most of the employers that left, left knowing that we had done everything we could for them, and that the decision had been based to decrease our workforce for nothing more than a genuine business reason and everyone understood what this was, even if they did not like it

It could have been a very different outcome.

Sites such as Glassdoor give interview candidates and employees the unprecedented opportunity to share the inside scoop on what it is *really* like to interview or work at a particular workplace; and this is leaving many employers feeling more than a little uncomfortable at the prospect of receiving public negative reviews.

One example of a company receiving less than glowing feedback on Glassdoor was Technorati.com, after a recent decision by its CEO to close its contributed content program in an effort to rebrand. According to multiple reviews on Glassdoor, many longtime contributors to Technorati.com were abruptly terminated, without thanks, respect, or appreciation.

Many reviews from these employees and contributors reference Technorati's CEO as the reason the company is "a sinking ship" and "taking a rapid nose dive."

So, how does this sort of feedback affect future recruiting and business growth? According to research into consumers' use of online reviews, 88 percent of people have been influenced by an online customer service review. And while the research into how online company reviews impact employee job decisions does not reveal quite the same degree of influence, we do know that a significant number of job seekers rely on these sites when evaluating a potential workplace.

In one study, for instance, out of 4,633 random job seekers surveyed, 48 percent had used Glassdoor at some point in their job search. The study also found that 60 percent of job seekers would not apply to a company with a one-star rating (on a five-point scale).

This suggests that many job seekers do seem to use workplace review sites, and negative reviews can dissuade them from applying to a particular company, and just as consumers now heavily rely on the reviews of products before purchasing, sites such as Glassdoor may only continue to gain momentum when it comes to new employees deciding on their next role and the company they want to work for. How you treat existing employees is, therefore, going to be an important part of how you protect your brand and your reputation, going forward, particularly if you want to be seen as an employer of choice.

Before you move on and look at the overarching factors, consider the following;

- Does the way you exit employees reflect your brand?
- Would it excite you as a potential employee?
- What would be different if you could wave a magic wand and create the best way for your people to be exited?
- How could you then implement this in your organization?

Then, answer:

- Does this allow your people to demonstrate their ability and a level of trust?

- Does it encourage ideas, creativity, and innovation for employees?
- Does it reflect that your people are individuals?
- Does it demonstrate that your people are leaders?
- Does it demonstrate that your people have a shared purpose, a shared vision, and shared values, and would it be something that they would feel proud about sharing with their family and friends?

Take some time to answer these questions and share your responses with your team and or your senior leaders.

Summary

We have covered a lot so far in the book (and we are not done yet), so let us quickly recap what the key themes are so far when it comes to implementing AGILE HR.

AGILE HR should:

- allow space for your employees to demonstrate their ability in a trusting and autonomous way
- encourage ideas, creativity, and innovation for your people
- demonstrate that your people are individuals
- demonstrate that your people are leaders
- reflect a shared purpose, a shared vision, and shared values that you would feel proud about sharing with your family and friends?

It is about openness, honesty, and trust, and furthermore, adult-to-adult conversations.

CHAPTER 5

Overarching Factors

As I said at the beginning of the book, there are some overarching factors when it comes to creating AGILE HR practices that should be considered, which we will look at in this chapter.

These factors are highlighted to provide an awareness of things that you should consider when looking to implement AGILE HR, and some of these factors are also things that can hinder and slow the progress that you want to make in your organization when it comes to doing things differently.

The factors that we will cover here are:

- Leadership
- Customers
- Your People
- Culture
- Diversity and Inclusion
- Financial
- Insight and Data
- Legislation
- Change

There may also be others that you can think of that may relate to your particular organization or sector.

5.1   Leadership

I mentioned leadership earlier in the book, and I want to cover it in more detail here and also break it down into two categories:

The leaders in your organization and

Your role as the HR leader in your organization.

The Leaders in Your Organization

How do they feel about HR initiatives?

Is HR a valued function in the business?

Do they understand the importance of the people in the organization?

Do they get on board with new initiatives quickly?

Unfortunately, many of the senior HR professionals that I work with still experience the senior leaders in their organization as the biggest blocker when it comes to trying to implement innovative people initiatives. For some, the most innovative thing is a new dress code policy that the CEO has asked for—how exciting, NOT!

As HR leaders, if we want to create a sustainable future for the HR profession, we have to get better at influencing and demonstrating to senior leaders that we know what we are talking about, and coaching them to our way of thinking.

Many senior leaders come from a place of old-school command and control type leadership and have not yet been able to cross the line into seeing the importance of letting people work with autonomy and treating them as adults. They are still of the mind that people are paid to follow instructions and do their job. This works for some, but we are seeing less and less of this type of leadership.

The difficulty for those that want to change is that they know they need to be doing things differently, but they do not know where to start. And this is where we need to step in.

We need to be pushing back when we are asked to design another long-winded policy to make up for yet another management shortfall. We need to be demonstrating that our people want something different, and that while we may not have all of the answers (when you try something new, you do not always get it right), by taking small (or *enormous* if you like) steps forward, things will start to get better.

I wrote a blog not too long ago about not disrupting HR as seems to be common phrase at the moment, but about disrupting leadership.

HR can produce the newest, most innovative, most amazing initiatives in the world, but if the leaders do not get on board with them, they will never work. Leaders need to lead and managers need to manage; without this, it will not matter how far you try and take things forward; you will always end up doing the same thing you have been doing for years and wondering why your employees are still not engaging with you.

Most leaders want to look at the financial side of what we are proposing, and we need to get better at this (more on this later), but we also need to be able to demonstrate value added, outside of the money side of things.

Removing annual performance reviews has been a topic that has been being discussed for a few years now, and LinkedIn is full of people sharing that they have stopped doing these. This is great in some ways as it shows that bell curves no longer seem to be the only way for us to manage performance; it also shows that leaders are starting to be open-minded to HR changes. But, it also brings into question whether annual reviews are only being stopped because nobody likes them doing them in the first place and it will free up more management time, one less way of speaking with and engaging our people that we do not need to worry about.

I mentioned earlier that stripping out annual reviews is great if you have a learning culture, or accountability for development and objectives already sits with your individual employees, but if not, you could be setting yourself up to fail on a magnificent scale, and you may find yourself out of a job or re-introducing annual reviews to help manage performance and set objectives.

The leaders need to acknowledge their role in supporting HR in driving and implementing changes; without this, do we have a sustainable future?

Your Role As the HR Leader in the Organization

Whether or not you are one of the HR professionals that struggles to get the senior leaders on board with what you are trying to do, your role in driving change across the business and with your team is critical when it comes to doing HR differently.

As HR professionals, we have been indoctrinated into our profession. We have been taught and trained on how to create policy after policy and how to ensure that these are followed without question.

We are the ones that have created the nine-box grids, the performance reviews, the dress code policies, the recruitment processes, the induction processes, probably all, if not most, of the HR processes and procedures that your business currently utilizes. And now, now you have realized that there is another way of delivering HR; you are in a position where you need to get the business on board, and your team members.

Your team members may be reluctant to make changes, given that this will be something they have not done before. Some may not know where to start; some may not want to step out of their comfort zone; some may be fearful; and your role will be to bring your team on the journey with you, while at the same time, managing the expectations of the wider business and the senior leaders.

The good news is that when your senior leaders and your HR team do get on board with this new way of doing things, you will be able to implement successful and sustainable change quickly in a way that will be more simple for you and your people.

That's exciting stuff.

5.2   Customers

Just as we looked at two different areas of leadership, we will look at two areas of customers—your internal and your external customers.

Internal Customers

You will have a number of internal customers and perhaps a number of stakeholders—the board, leaders, other departments, managers, existing employees, and new employees. Perhaps you also outsource some of your recruitment, payroll and so on, and you have these relationships to manage as well.

How could an AGILE approach to HR help?

Employees will have greater responsibility for their own career journey, meaning they are responsible for their learning, their objectives, their performance, and their career progression. This gives managers more time to coach and develop their people or even people from other business areas.

On the whole, you will have less performance issues to deal with and more time to focus on the strategic, innovative, exciting parts of HR.

Business performance will improve, customer satisfaction will improve, your employees will be engaged, you will be adding value and saving money and you will be creating a sustainable future for HR.

External Customers

For many of your customers, AGILE HR practices may work in their favor considerably. Imagine trusting that your employees come to work each day to do a good job and that you trust them and allow them to work with autonomy, how could that be of benefit to your customers?

How many complaints could you resolve quickly if your people were trusted enough to say sorry, or send a bunch of flowers? How many complaints and issues would not escalate if your people could make a decision instead of following a process that means they cannot go any further with this at this point, but will escalate and get someone to look into it for them?

How much management time would you save if your people did not have to refer everything to their manager when a £50 gift card or just a card with an apology would do the trick?

LEGO is a great example of how to keep your customers happy—you will find some more details on this in the Resources section.

5.3   Your People

Your people will likely be the biggest thing to consider when it comes to doing things differently and considering an AGILE approach to HR. I cannot stress enough how vital engaging with your people will be to your success.

As we have touched on throughout the book, many of the current ways of working involve the HR team shutting themselves away in a room and designing "People Solutions" in isolation.

What the neuroscience tells us, though, is that this is not working, and we see it in practice.

If you continue to exclude your people in finding the best way to do things, it will continue not to work. You will never get to a position where you can please all of the people all of the time, and this is not what you should try and focus on, but before you go and remove your performance management system, ask your people what they want. Some people will welcome an annual appraisal because it is the only time they have interaction and feedback with their manager, so do not just take it away because that is what everyone is doing at this current time.

Spend time engaging with your people, in ways other than another survey, and have conversations about why they joined, why they have stayed, what they love, what they would like to see changed, what would make their roles easier, how they want to develop, how they want to be thanked, and so on.

Your people will allow you to gain the insight you need, in order for you to design and develop solutions that are right for your people and your business.

Whenever we work with clients, we always look at where we can interact with employees and gain their views to help create the right solution. We could, of course, design in isolation whatever the client wants us to design, but how will we know if it is going to be the right solution, unless we ask the questions of the people who will be implementing it and using it in their role?

5.4   Culture

Culture plays a big part in when and how you implement AGILE HR, if at all. I love the Tribal Leadership framework on culture change and how there are five stages of culture. You know where you are, based on the language, relationships, and the behavior. If your organization is totally command and control and your people are referred to as assets, and if people are never on the agenda or are skipped over at every board meeting, then you may have a tougher job than those who are willing to change and accept risk. Risk aversion does not help AGILE HR. But if you can get people on board and involve your employees with the design of whatever you want to change, making sure you do not end up creating another process, then you will be onto a winner. You may also be able to find some quick wins, although as we have discussed already, real change takes time. I do not suggest just scrapping something altogether and hoping it works.

5.5 Diversity and Inclusion

When dealing with people, as well as them being individuals, there are also the considerations of gender, race, religion, disability, sexuality, age and so on. Adult-to-adult conversations require trust and if that is lacking because the x group always get treated more/less favorably, then tread carefully. How you communicate the message will be critical, and trusting managers to choose their own pay grades, or to award individuals for great work could be seen as unfair to some, regardless of protected characteristics. But coming back to the risk factor, you may well get some complaints from your people when you scrap a certain long and complicated process, because even though it is not right, it may be deemed fair.

5.6 Financial

Understand your figures if you want to make a change so that you have a better chance of gaining buy-in from those who focus on the money. All too often, an initiative that will improve customer satisfaction or a new product that will win new customers and lots of profits will be agreed to without the need for it to be tried and tested; sadly when it comes to our people, unless you can back it up with evidence or you know it is been tried and tested elsewhere, it is unlikely you will get past the post.

5.7 Insight and Data (Include data blog)

This is a biggie for a lot of HR professionals. I do not know about you, but rarely have I felt confident with the data I am presenting, I usually have a caveat of some sorts because x manager has not met with us yet, or finance are still validating, or the system is so ineffective that we are having to manually manipulate the data and we need to allow for human error. If we want to be seen as HR professionals that can hold our own, whether moving to an AGILE approach or not, we have to get better, much better with insight and data.

5.8 Legislation

We are surrounded by legislation, from Health and Safety to Employment Legislation, Financial, Data Protection; it is an ongoing and never ending list and it is not, I believe, going to get any easier. And in some cases, it should not, but just as we have seen throughout the book, when it comes to policy and legislation, this is largely brought in because of one serious issue that has arisen, and everyone then needs to tighten their belts and adhere to the new rules.

It is important that you understand the legislation that surrounds your sector/company and ensure that you remain compliant with anything you are trying to change.

It may not be just statute that you have to follow either. A sector that I have been working with recently has to manage the performance of their employees on an annual basis in order to justify spend, meet the requirements of trustees and meet government expectations, so removing the annual performance reviews is not an option (currently) for this client, but that does not mean we cannot improve the process and make it more beneficial for the employees and their managers.

So, understand what your constraints are, and work within, or around these before you promise the earth to people.

5.9   Change

Change is the one constant in business today, and should be considered before you embark on a new HR initiative.

Just last week, a large retailer in the UK announced to the press that over the next two years, they would increase store employee salaries by 10.5 percent; this was on the same day that they announced internally that there would be a 25 percent cut in head office employees—not a great move!

So, consider when you make changes, but do not allow change to stop you in your tracks. I have seen so many times organizations hold back on restructuring announcements while they wait for the "right time." There is no right time to announce this, although I would suggest not making the announcement on the same day as you go the press about salary increases. You also probably do not want to announce your new talent management program on the same day that you start consultation on reducing the number of managers in the business.

Engage people in the changes, whatever you are changing. Change is more successful when you can get your people to see what is in it for them, when they can really see that it will benefit them, make things easier for them. Just telling them this is not really going to help. You need to change the hearts and minds if you want any change—no matter how big or small—to be successful.

CHAPTER 6

Putting It into Practice

6.1   How Do We Create Change?

Here are a few things you can do to start to get the conversations going and begin to implement AGILE HR in your organization:

- Explore the AGILE model with your team and your leaders to get them on board with the thinking and the possibilities of what you could create
- Be realistic with the scope and scale of what you are wanting to do differently, taking into consideration the overarching factors
- Pilot your changes with end users, selecting maybe just one team for a period
- Build your case for change using both qualitative and quantitative data
- Ensure that you are addressing the needs of your organization, not just those areas that are underperforming
- Build in regular sense checks and reviews
- Focus on building your leaders' skills, knowledge, and abilities
- Look at the shape, size, and strengths of your HR function and see if you need to make changes to reflect a more AGILE approach.

6.2   The HR Function of the Future

What does an HR function of the future need to do?

There is so much discussion at the moment about the future of HR, and indeed, if HR even has a future. Personally, I am involved with groups online and in person, talking about not only about the structure, but about the skills that we need to have.

So, what are these conversations telling us about the future of HR? Here are the five most common topics currently:

Insight

We need to be skilled and more equipped at gathering, interpreting, and using data to help us inform the business on the strategic direction of the HR function. And we need to use this data to define what we will and will not be focusing on. Changing the name of the function with no change to the way in which we operate and with no real insight into why this will have a positive impact on the organization, other than because everyone else is doing it, is not going to help HR survive. Concrete data, greater insight into the people activities, costs, and how to implement efficiencies, cost savings, and drive performance improvements is what is needed.

Research and Development

We have talked about this before and we are becoming aware that innovation in customer activity is one thing; it gives your company a competitive edge and keeps the money coming in, yet when it comes to new thinking for your own people, innovation gets boxed, until evidence can be provided as to why something new should be tried (back to insight). But if you really want the edge when it comes to your people, and you want to be an employer of choice where the talented people want to work, then you need to stay one step ahead of the game. R&D will play a crucial role in this. What is on the horizon? What would give your company the edge? What new thinking or new ways of engaging, leading, and motivating people are taking place in businesses right now?

Embedded into the Business

Matrix management seems to be a hot topic of conversation at the moment. Business partnering, when it works effectively is great, yet in some cases, we have given the title of BP without the accountability of authority to go with it. Whether organizations move to self-managing teams or not, matrix management for HR and indeed other central functions, removes the one-size-fits-all approach and ensures that people solutions are right for the individuals, the business unit, and therefore, the business as a whole.

Human-Focused

Finally, let us actually get the Human back into Human Resources. The HR function of the future needs to stop being a police department and actually focus on the needs of the people in the business, while of course, still keeping an eye on strategic objectives and business needs. The HR team should not be limited in their contact with HR, that is, recruitment, disciplinary, grievance, and exit. If HR is truly interested in designing and implementing solutions that are right for the employees and the business, then positive, regular engagement needs to take place.

Agile

HR needs to be better at moving with technology, responding to the needs of the business and its customers. It needs to be able to flex, and adapt, and listen, and communicate, and be able to find solutions instead of thinking about why things cannot be done. HR needs to be able to work with minimum policies that are compliant, yet simple and flexible, yet understood. We need to throw away what worked 30 years ago, and speak to people to find out what they really need. Involved in these conversations are organizations, large and small, and the internal conversations that appear to be taking place are about more learning and OD and less HR.

Will these five things ensure there is an HR of the future, or have we left it too late?

What are your thoughts?

What is missing from the thinking?

What do you see as the priorities?

CHAPTER 7

Diagnostic Introduction

At Chrysalis Consulting, we have designed a diagnostic tool to help you establish whether you are already operating an AGILE[1] approach to HR in your organization, which you can find on our website: http://www.chrysalis-consulting.co.uk/agile-hr/

Our thinking behind this is to get you looking at things differently, and for the most part, when people complete this, they are able to ascertain just from the questions whether their existing approach is fit for purpose, and then, receive a bespoke report based on their answers.

Here, you can take a look at the questions for yourself, and if you want the report, just complete the diagnostic online and you will have something to talk to your team and your leaders about.

Employees As Able

This first series of statements looks at whether you see your employees as adults able to work autonomously and to a high standard—or whether you micromanage them and use a series of policies as strict guidelines on how they should act, feel, and behave in case things go wrong.

1. Our people policies tell our people what we expect from them.
   versus
   Our people policies are designed around what our people have told us they need to know to do their jobs well.

---

[1]Our AGILE HR diagnostic has been produced based on the thinking and methodology of the EACH (Employees as Adults, Consumers and Human Beings model) created by Disruptive HR.

2. Our training programs are scheduled throughout the year.

   versus

   Our people learn at the point where they identify the need and at times that work best for them.

3. We manage our internal communications through scripted cascades.

   versus

   We provide the bare bones of the content and allow managers a lot of discretion and interpretation of the messaging.

4. We tend to produce new rules in response to things going wrong.

   versus

   When things go wrong, we look at individual behavior and deal with that, rather than producing a new rule.

5. Many of our processes exist because if we did not have them, our managers would not engage and lead properly.

   versus

   We do not create processes around poor leaders.

6. We have a fairly linear career path for progression.

   versus

   We have a flexible approach to career paths. People can dial up/down or move sideways freely.

7. The key purpose of our induction is telling new employees what is expected of them.

   versus

   The key purpose of our induction is to find out the individual talents and strengths of our new employees.

8. We allocate performance ratings as part of our performance management system.

   versus

   We do not rate or grade our employees as part of our approach to performance management.

9. We promote our managers based on their technical ability and their commitment to the business.

   versus

   We recruit managers with the right behaviors and skills to lead and manage a team.

10. We rarely check out how our people policies are being received by our people.

    versus

    We regularly get feedback from employees on how they feel about our people policies and make changes as a result.

11. We categorize our talent through a nine-box grid so we can identify the high potentials.

    versus

    We do not categorize our people in terms of their potential. Our focus is on helping all employees stretch and fulfil their potential.

Game-Changing Employees

This series of statements looks at how your employees work, lead, create, and innovate differently to that of your competitors in an open, honest, and transparent way—or whether you prefer a more traditional approach with set guidelines and information for your people to follow.

12. Our social media policy is quite strict about how people can use it as we worry about the risks of misuse and how this could impact on our brand.

    versus

    We encourage our people to use social media as we recognize the potential value to our brand.

13. We are careful about what we tell our employees.

    versus

    We tend to be as transparent as we can in what we tell our employees.

14. We have clear guidelines about what people can be paid, based on strict grading criteria and performance grades.

    versus

    Our line managers use a lot of discretion to work out pay and bonuses.

15. Rewards are given by managers.

    versus

    Employees nominate each other for rewards.

16. We believe in paying for performance and incentivizing people to work harder/smarter.

    versus

    We do not believe money is the key motivator.

17. We have an annual bonus scheme.

    versus

    Our managers make "spot" rewards (either in pay or non-cash/gift voucher) when they feel someone has done something great.

18. We split rewards between base pay and a discretionary element.

    versus

    We pay our people well and do not have a discretionary element.

19. Our people policies protect the business from employee errors.

    versus

    We understand why employees have made errors and offer support and development as part of our culture of learning.

20. We ask for ideas for improvements at set times throughout the year, and then, design projects to implement these.

    versus

    We encourage fresh ideas, new ways of working, and an entrepreneurial spirit.

Employees As Individuals

This series of statements asks whether you place your people at the heart of what you do in HR by valuing the differences of your people or whether you tend toward HR approaches that ignore how people think, feel, behave, learn, and are engaged and motivated and believe a one-size-fits all approach is best for your organization.

21. We have a leadership competency model.

    versus

    We focus on the existing strengths of our leaders and work with those.

22. Our induction is based on what we need our employees to know.

    versus

    Our employees create our induction, based on what would have been useful to them when they started.

23. Our leadership development is focused on getting them to learn a pre-identified set of competencies.

    versus

    We work with our leaders to help them know themselves better. We believe that if they know themselves well, they make better leaders.

24. Our leadership development is focused on the technical aspects of leadership.

    versus

    We focus on helping leaders "be themselves better," that is: giving them the confidence to show humility, authenticity, integrity, tell personal stories, say thanks and so on.

25. We expect our employees to act in line with our culture, values, and behavioral frameworks at all times.

    versus

    We encourage employees to be themselves at work, recognizing that in order for them to be working with us, some of our core values must be aligned.

26. We have a limited range of rewards.

    versus

    Rewards in our organization are very personalized, based on what people really want.

27. We have a high potential program.

    versus

    We tailor our talent management to the individual needs and wants of each employee.

28. We assess our candidates against a clear job specification and train them to do the job to meet our requirements.

    versus

    We use the recruitment process to identify their strengths, and then, fit the job around them, recognizing that we all have different strengths.

Employees As Leaders

This series of statements looks at how your people collaborate, lead, and succeed in their roles—or whether leadership is considered to be a position you hold.

29. Our structure reflects the levels we need to operate efficiently, with designated operational teams and functions.

    versus

    Our structure is agile and reflects matrix management, which meets the flexible needs of our organization.

30. Responsibility for performance management sits with our managers.

    versus

    Employees are responsible for managing their own performance.

31. Our most senior employees are the only leaders within the business.

    versus

    We recognize that leadership is much more than a position you hold.

32. We do top–down succession planning.

    versus

    We "crowd source" our future leaders through getting the views of our people.

33. Our induction is a program delivered to groups of new starters.

    versus

    Our induction is a blend of activities and a set of resources that employees can access as and when they need them.

34. We have training programs for our employees.

    versus

    We provide access to a range of different learning resources so that our people can learn in ways to suit them.

35. Our people policies are designed to protect the organization from the poor behavior of individuals.

    versus

    Our people policies are designed on the assumption that people come to work to do a good job and behave well.

36. We provide leadership development programs.

    versus

    We encourage leaders to develop themselves.

37. We want great managers who can manage the day-to-day needs of the team.

    versus

    Our managers coach their teams, allowing them to work with autonomy.

38. We measure the performance of our people through strict measures as well as looking at their time in the business.

    versus

    We measure outputs, not hours worked.

39. Our induction is a self-contained program.

    versus

    Our induction informs how we manage and engage our individual employees.

40. We have forced or guided distribution of ratings as we believe this ensures performance differentiation.

    versus

    We do not have any forced or guided distribution as we do not believe this enables better performance.

41. We create our people policies and processes within the HR function.

    versus

    We involve our employees in the creation of our people policies and processes.

Employees Are Engaged

This final series of statements asks whether you place your people at the heart of what you do in HR or whether you tend toward HR approaches that ignore how people think, feel, behave, learn, and are engaged, and motivated.

42. We advertise our vacancies and see who is interested.

    versus

    We have a community of people on our radar who we keep engaged and target potential candidates.

43. Our people policies are very detailed and specific.

    versus

    Our people policies allow for our employees to use their own judgment.

44. Our leadership communications tend to be quite formal.

    versus

    Our leadership communications allow for individual personalities.

45. Our leadership conferences tend to be PowerPoint-heavy and broadcast in style.

    versus

    We rarely use PowerPoint. Our leadership conferences are story-based and highly interactive.

46. People are thanked through the bonus they get.

    versus

    We regularly say "Thank You" in lots of small ways—gifts, hand-written notes, phone calls and so on.

47. We want our employees to focus purely on doing their job to the best of their ability.

    versus

    We welcome fresh ideas and entrepreneurial thinking and believe this helps us create a great place to work and grow.

48. We have a "probation" period.

    versus

    We have a "test it out" period.

49. Our approaches to recruitment, training and so on tend to be quite formal and traditional.

    versus

    We use games, competitions, and so on a lot in how we recruit, develop, and engage our people.

50. Our people are engaged, mostly based on how we reward them and recognize their achievements

    versus

    We recognize that our people are engaged most when they have meaning and purpose to their work

51. We do an annual (bi-annual) engagement survey.

    versus

    We seek out our people's views/feelings frequently and in a wide variety of ways.

CHAPTER 8

Case Studies

In this section, you will find examples of work carried out by Chrysalis Consulting for some of our clients that might give you some ideas on how to do things differently.

Case Study 1
LEADing the Way

Why?

Our London-based client with a workforce of 3,500 approached us about delivering a Leadership Development Program for 100 of their leaders who were looking to be better leaders. The HR director had participated in our program for HR leaders and wanted to offer this to the leadership population as a different way of learning to help leaders better engage, lead, and motivate their teams.

What?

We worked with the HRD and CEO to understand any specific needs of the business and how best to deliver the program to ensure engagement and motivation for learning. We then worked with the HRD to design a short questionnaire for the participants so that we could ensure we met their individual needs and objectives; we repeated this again 6 months into the program.

The program included four 2-day workshops, one-to-one coaching and some online learning content. The 12-month program focused on the areas of Self: Be More, Relationships: Have more, Work: Do more, and World: Give more.

To allow time and space for embedding the learning, every participant had an additional "time to think" day every month as well as being able to use real-life examples of projects, goals, or objectives relevant to their business area so that the changes were seen and felt across the organization.

Pulse surveys were carried out with employees across the organization before, during, and after the program to sense check the changes and measure the growth of the leaders, the impact on the employees, and the success of the company.

Outcome

By the end of the program, employees reported that they felt more valued, leaders reported that they felt more in control and more comfortable in their roles, and the organization saw an increase in performance, customer satisfaction, and profits.

Case Study 2

Putting People First

Why?

Our London-based client with 1,200 employees approached us after the appointment of a new CEO and HRD to provide some additional support to the HR function following three consecutive restructures and a significant decrease in engagement, productivity, and performance.

What?

We worked closely with both the HRD and CEO to identify their vision and aspirations for the organization and the HR function and looked at where to focus in the short-, long-, and medium-term. The lack of engagement had occurred due to a breakdown in trust between the senior team and managers, which was directly impacting employees. Engagement workshops were held with the managers and senior leaders to find ways in which to work together more effectively.

The role of the executive team members was redefined, managers given more responsibility and greater autonomy, and further solutions were identified and implemented over the next 12 months. A new People function was implemented, and a greater partnership model was put in place. A new People strategy was created, ensuring it was aligned to business, financial, and performance goals. Policies and procedures were simplified, some even being removed completely, and employees began to comment that they felt more trusted and empowered to do their job.

The vision and values were relaunched and workshops were led by employee ambassadors who wanted to help to drive and champion change.

Outcome

12 months later, and the business has grown from strength to strength. Customer satisfaction and employee engagement have increased significantly and sickness levels have decreased for the first time in 5 years.

Case Study 3
Saving Time and Money

Why?

Our client, a leading logistics company, contacted us about helping with some cost saving activities. One site closure and one site relocating in a short space of time and savings needed to be found in other bases.

What?

Closing one site is difficult; another coupled with a relocation was tough. Utilizing our experience in "People," we ensured those affected by redundancy were supported from CV writing through to 1-2-1s on interview techniques. Relocation required engaging stakeholders, both internally and externally, ensuring all aspects were covered from IT through to ensuring we had canteen facilities—colleagues need to be fed and watered!

Outcome

Closure saw all but one colleague either continuing their employment at a different location or being successful in securing employment locally elsewhere. Relocation wise was deemed as Zero impact to customer and a seamless transition from one site to the next. Huge success!

Case Study 4
The HR Function

Why?

Our Peterborough-based start-up IT security company was growing and in need of some support in reviewing, designing, and implementing their HR policies and procedures. The company was 2 years old, started with five founding directors, and was now recruiting an increasing number of employees.

What?

We worked with them in understanding their short-, medium-, and long-term needs and growth plans as well as understanding more about the type of culture and environment they wanted to create for their people.

We reviewed and added to their employee handbook, designed and implemented a performance management framework and induction process, and carried out some initial management training for the senior team as well as carried out annual reviews of all contracts and policies.

Latterly, we have worked with them on streamlining some of their processes to free up management time and have helped with strategic people planning to ensure the right people are recruited in the right roles at the right time.

Outcome

The senior team are now more confident in dealing with recruitment, induction, and performance management and deal with any issues quickly and effectively as and when they arise. We have developed a fantastic partnership with the client, know their team, their aspirations, and their growth plans, and are on hand by phone and e-mail at any time as well as provide face-to-face support and attend company social events.

Case Study 5

Blended Learning

Why Blended Learning?

Our London-based client with 3,000 employees had been engaging with staff and identified that they wanted to offer online learning to their workforce after implementing agile working across their four sites. This would allow employees to learn in their own time and offer a greater number of courses.

What?

We worked with them to identify the types of courses they wanted to offer online, the theme, style, and length and also to understand if they wanted to complement any of the existing face-to-face courses and programs. Their biggest concern about moving to online, despite it being requested by their employees, was that learning would not be embedded and that people would be learning in isolation. We discussed with them our interactive learning system that encourages collaboration, social learning, and social interaction and the "I commit to . . ." at the end of the course, where people share what they will change/do as a result of the course.

The courses we designed included some of our existing courses as well as some of the organization's existing content. Three courses were created jointly, taking into account the needs of the business to complement the induction process for new employees as well as offering this to existing employees. The content of the course topics varied from mandatory training, personal development courses, and professional development courses.

Outcome

Engagement with learning improved, whilet the learning spend decreased. Employees commented that they could learn what they needed when they needed it and could go back for refresher courses when needed. They also loved the fact that they could learn at home, on the train, and at times to suit them.

Case Study 6

Changing Mindsets

Why?

A senior HR professional approached us about some coaching support. It was to help increase confidence, improve relationships, and influence skills so they felt able to apply for an HR director position.

What?

Kelly met with them initially to fully understand their needs and ideal outcomes by the end of the coaching relationship. By the end of the first session, the client had let go and released some negative thought patterns. They had stemmed from school and early work experiences that had caused some self-doubt and self-limiting beliefs in their own ability. The client agreed on some actions to take forward and made a commitment to make a change and have a "challenging" conversation the next day.

By the second session, the client appeared visibly more confident and focused on the amazing changes that they had made since the first session. They came prepared with their own agenda for the session and were more determined than ever to move their career forward. They also noted that relationships out of work were also improved, that they were sleeping better, and really focusing on the positives. They commented that the changes had happened so quickly they could not believe they had not considered this type of coaching before.

Outcome

Within 4 months, the client secured a new role, with a new and much larger organization in a more senior position as HR director. They even negotiated their remuneration package to secure a higher salary (something they never thought they would be able to do).

They were happier, more confident, and more relaxed and engaged with us to work with three of their new team members.

Case Study 7

Keeping Things Simple

Why?

Our Norfolk-based client with a workforce of 2,700 employees approached us about supporting them in simplifying their behavior framework to help it come to life more in the organization. The existing framework was long, complicated, and difficult for employees at all levels to understand and implement in their day-to-day roles.

What?

A lot of engagement had been carried out internally with employees, employee forums, and leaders to highlight what was important and what was needed moving forward.

We then facilitated a workshop with employees, leaders, directors, and trustees to discuss the work so far, the need for change, the five stages of culture and how to implement change in the organization.

Collating all of the information, we produced a behavior framework in one simple visual, a "behavior dictionary" to provide more detail when recruiting, inducting, developing, and leading employees, based on the compassionate leadership model and focused on all employees, taking accountability for their words, actions, role, and development.

Outcome

All employees, including trustees, were delighted with the results, communication and the culture improved, and the expectations of employees were understood and delivered by all employees in a relatively short amount of time. The framework was also integrated into all other areas of the employee life cycle and became an integral part of the way they do things, focusing on doing things differently.

Case Study 8

Performance Reviews—What Next?

Why?

Our global client with over 10,000 employees contacted us about helping them improve the performance review process in the UK and Europe. The process had become a laborious tick box exercise with little value added, and they wanted to do something different. They had heard about the work we had done with one of their competitors and wanted a fresh approach.

What?

We worked in partnership with the senior leadership to understand the requirements of their business areas, the culture across the different sites and countries, as well as observing the way in which employees worked with one another, and then, provided three solutions.

The desired solution was to remove performance appraisals from the business, but to find ways to improve performance and ensure that employees felt valued. Introducing a learning culture into the organization seemed to be the priority, meaning that employees would be more accountable for their learning, development, goals, and objectives.

Coaching and mentoring were implemented, managers began to provide on-the-spot rewards, including Thank You cards, lunch vouchers, and monetary rewards, and employees took responsibility for their own development. Work shadowing, internal and external secondments and online bite-size learning were introduced internally as well as trusting employees to purchase courses, books, and programs to help them develop in their roles and build on their skills.

Outcome

Two years in, and retention and engagement have improved, as have customer service and business performance.

The organization pulse check employees through short surveys and hold regular engagement workshops with employees at all levels to identify further changes as part of their continuous improvement plan and they are delighted that they took the risk to do things differently.

CHAPTER 9

Resources

We have got lots of information in different styles and formats to help you understand and implement AGILE HR in your organization. We want to make this as accessible to as many people as possible to help create a sustainable future for the HR function and allow you to do things differently.

View the webinar at: https://www.youtube.com/watch?v=vp9wH3GWYwk&t=649s

Complete the diagnostic at: http://www.chrysalis-consulting.co.uk/diagnostic-tool/

Buy the online program at: http://www.chrysalis-consulting.co.uk/agile-hr/

Attend a workshop at: http://www.chrysalis-consulting.co.uk/agile-hr/

Or, contact us about delivering an in-house session for your HR team and senior leaders at: mail@chrysalis-consulting.co.uk

CHAPTER 10

Summary—Reflections

AGILE HR does not have to be hard, but we do have to focus on changing our own mindsets and that of our teams and organizations.

We need to be the people experts and not a transactional service, although of course, there will be transactions that need to be made.

AGILE HR should:

- allow space for your employees to demonstrate their ability in a trusting and autonomous way
- encourage ideas, creativity, and innovation for your people
- demonstrate that your people are individuals
- demonstrate that your people are leaders
- reflect a shared purpose, a shared vision, and shared values that you would feel proud about sharing with your family and friends?

I have been implementing AGILE now for over 5 years and it really does make a difference to employees. It stops or at least reduces the Monday-to-Friday dying syndrome that I highlighted in the Introduction and engages people more in the work that they do, which ultimately improves performance of the person and the business.

I love making a difference and I do believe that we need to be engaged and working with a purpose in order for us to feel fulfilled in all areas of our lives. The workplace is where we spend more than half of our lives; AGILE HR can help us enjoy it.

Index

Adult-to-adult conversations, 77
AGILE HR, 5, 21–24, 77, 85
  employees. *See* employees
  implementing, 81
  practices, overarching factors. *See*
    overarching factors, AGILE
    HR practices
Anger, 11
Annual bonus scheme, 88
Annual (bi-annual) engagement
  survey, 92
Annual performance reviews, 48,
  73, 78
Anxiety, 10, 11, 12
Appraisals
  performance, 100–101
  process, 48
Attitudes, 66

Behavior, 13
  dictionary, 99
  framework, 99
  patterns of, 11
Blended learning, 97–98
Boxes, 55
Business, needs of, 93

Career coaching, 54
Case studies, 93–102
Change, 78–79
Chrysalis Consulting, 15, 28, 45, 53,
  85, 93
CIPD, 38
  absence management survey, 36
Coaching, 47, 100–101
  career, 54
Communications, 62–66
Competency-based interview, 27, 29
Competency-based questioning, 26

Corporate induction, 32, 33
Courses, 97–98
Culture, 76
Customer, 74–75
  external, 75
  internal, 74–75
  satisfaction, 95
  service advisor, 54

Data, 77
Department of Health (DoH)
  research, 36–37
Depression, 11
Diversity, 77
Dress code policies, 73–74

Effective leadership, 6
Effective management, 6
Employee life cycle, 25
  engagement and communications,
    62–66
  exit, 66–70
  leadership development, 56–61
  learning and development, 44–48
  onboarding/induction, 30–35
  performance management, 48–51
  recruitment, 25–30
  reward, 41–44
  talent management, 51–55
  well-being, 35–41
Employees, 6, 98
  as able, 22, 85–87
  engaged/engagement, 5, 22–23,
    91–92, 95, 101
  feedback form, 63
  forums, 99
  game-changing, 22, 87–88
  as individuals, 22, 88–89
  as leaders, 22, 89–91

Employees (*Continued*)
  performance of, 50
  training programs for, 90
Employee well-being, 36, 39
  factor in, 38–39
Employment, 96. *See also* Employees
  legislation, 7–8
Employment tribunals (ETs), 8, 32
Engaged employees, 62–63
Engagement, 62–66
  workshops, 95, 101
Executive team members, role of, 95
Exit of employees, 66–70
External customers, 75

Face-to-face courses, 97–98
Fear-driven leadership, 16
Feedback, 63–64
Feminine leadership traits, 17–19
Finance, 29
Financial overarching factors, 77

Gerzema, John, 17
Grids, 55
Group assessment center, 26

Health and Safety Executive (HSE),
    36–37
HR. *See* Human resources (HR)
HR function of future, 81–82
  agile, 83
  embedded into business, 82–83
  human-focused, 83
  insight, 82
  research and development, 82
HSE. *See* Health and Safety
    Executive (HSE)
Human resources (HR)
  approaches, 88
  communities, 8
  function, 8, 94, 96–97
  leaders, program for, 93
  old-school styles of, 8
  policies and procedures, 96
  policy, 6
  practices, 6
  processes and procedures, 73–74

Inclusion, 77
Induction, 32, 73–74, 86, 88, 90,
    91, 96
  corporate, 32, 33
  definition of, 34
  design of, 35
  HR process for, 33
  "new and improved," 33
Initial management training, 96
Initiatives, 36
Insight, 77
Interactive learning system, 97–98
Internal communications, 86
Internal customers, 74–75
Internal processes, 30
Internships, 28
Interview, 25, 29
  experiences, 29
  panel, 28

Job market, 25
John Lewis Partnership, 51–52

Leaders/leadership, 6, 71–74, 93
  categories, 71
  common traits, 59
  communications, 91
  competency model, 88
  conferences, 92
  development, 56–61, 59, 61, 89,
      90, 93
  fear-driven, 16
  in organization, 72–73
  role, 73–74
  team suggestion, 64
  technical aspects of, 89
Learning, 44
  access to, 46
  blended, 97–98
  and development, 44–48
  engagement and motivation
      for, 93
Legislation, 77–78
LEGO, 27
Life balance, 35–36
Line managers, 39
LinkedIn, 73

Management thinking, 5, 17
Marks & Spencer, 39
Masculine leadership traits, 17–19
Meditation, 36
Mentor/mentoring, 35, 46, 100–101
Mindset, 9–14
  changing, 98–99
  scenario 1, 14
  scenario 2, 14–16
Monday-to-Friday dying syndrome,
    16, 19

Negative reviews, 69
Negative thinking, 12

Onboarding/induction, 30–35
One-to-one coaching, 94
Online learning content, 94
Online program, 41
Online working, 6
On-the-job training, 46
Organization, 7, 55
  vision and aspirations for, 94–95
Organizational well-being, 38, 40–41
Overarching factors, AGILE HR
    practices, 71
  change, 78–79
  culture, 76
  customers, 74–75
  diversity and inclusion, 77
  financial, 77
  insight and data, 77
  leadership, 71–74
  legislation, 77–78
  your people, 75–76

People strategy, 95
Performance
  appraisals, 100–101
  differentiation, 91
  of employees, 50
  grades, 87
  paying for, 88
  ratings, 86
  reviews, 73–74, 100–101
Performance management, 48–51, 54
  framework, 96

responsibility for, 90
system, 76
Personal development, 60
Personal well-being, 37, 40
  essential factors leading to, 38
Practice
  creating change, 81
  HR function of future,
    81–83
Primitive mind, 12
Procurement, 29
Professional development, 60
Programs, 36
Pulse surveys, 94

Radical change, 7
Rapid eye movement, 13
Recruitment, 25–30, 31,
    73–74, 92
  processes, 26–27
Redundancy process, 68
Relocation, 96
REM sleep, 13–14
Resources, 103
Reviews, performance, 100–101
Rewards, 41–44, 87
  limited range of, 89
  split, 88
Risk aversion, 76

Security, 62
Self-reflection, 47
Social context, 37
Social media policy, 87
Split rewards, 88
Sponsorship, 46
Stakeholders, expectations of, 29
Stress, 36

Talent management, 51–55, 54
Technology, 7
  and learning, 46
  use of, 36
360-degree performance review, 62
Tick box exercise, 49
Top-down succession planning, 90
Traffic delays, 31

Training programs, 86
    for employees, 90
Transport delays, 31
Tribal Leadership framework, 76

UK Government strategy for health, 39
Unemployment, 62

Well-being, 35–41
    employee, 39
    personal, 37
WFH. *See* Working from home (WFH)

Working from home (WFH), 5
    performance review, 5
    policies, 6–7
Working relationships, 38
Work-life balance, 35–36
Work shadowing, 101
Workshops, 41, 46, 94
    engagement, 95

Yoga, 36

Zappos workforce, 65

OTHER TITLES IN THE HUMAN RESOURCE MANAGEMENT AND ORGANIZATIONAL BEHAVIOR COLLECTION

- *Deconstructing Management Maxims, Volume I: A Critical Examination of Conventional Business Wisdom* by Kevin Wayne
- *Deconstructing Management Maxims, Volume II: A Critical Examination of Conventional Business Wisdom* by Kevin Wayne
- *The Real Me: Find and Express Your Authentic Self* by Mark Eyre
- *Across the Spectrum: What Color Are You?* by Stephen Elkins-Jarrett
- *The Human Resource Professional's Guide to Change Management: Practical Tools and Techniques to Enact Meaningful and Lasting Organizational Change* by Melanie J. Peacock
- *Tough Calls: How to Move Beyond Indecision and Good Intentions* by Linda D. Henman
- *Life of a Lifetime: Inspiration for Creating Your Extraordinary Life* by Christoph Spiessens
- *The Facilitative Leader: Managing Performance Without Controlling People* by Steve Reilly
- *The DNA of Leadership: Creating Healthy Leaders and Vibrant Organizations* by Myron Beard and Alan Weiss
- *Human Resources as Business Partner: How to Maximize the Value and Financial Contribution of HR* by Tony Miller

Announcing the Business Expert Press Digital Library

Concise e-books business students need for classroom and research

This book can also be purchased in an e-book collection by your library as

- a one-time purchase,
- that is owned forever,
- allows for simultaneous readers,
- has no restrictions on printing, and
- can be downloaded as PDFs from within the library community.

Our digital library collections are a great solution to beat the rising cost of textbooks. E-books can be loaded into their course management systems or onto students' e-book readers. The **Business Expert Press** digital libraries are very affordable, with no obligation to buy in future years. For more information, please visit **www.businessexpertpress.com/librarians**. To set up a trial in the United States, please email **sales@businessexpertpress.com**.